Living Awake
20 Techniques to End
"I Got It; I Lost It"

Lisa Carrillo

Published by Experiencing the True Self
Publishing

Living Awake:

20 Techniques to End "I Got It; I Lost It"

www.experiencingthetrueself.com

Cover design by Lisa Carrillo

Paperback:
ISBN 978-1-7371564-0-6

ebook:
ISBN 978-1-7371564-1-3

CONTENTS

Introduction

I t is no accident that you're reading these words right now.

You may have had glimpses of our true nature: you experience a causeless peace or joy and see that we aren't our bodies but a timeless, fearless essence. You know that all is well. It's like briefly tuning in to the frequency of backstage commands reaching actors' ear pieces, like hearing the deep rhythm carrying the universal dance.

Then, the clarity becomes murky. Either it seems to disappear altogether in the face of day-to-day challenges, or you find yourself acting and relating in ways that don't reflect this deeper knowing. This apparent contradiction is the "I got it; I lost it" phenomenon.

As tools, our brains help us interact with the world, but they are woefully inadequate to conceptualize our true nature and the preciousness of life. Sometimes we seem to be stuck in a dichotomy--feeling the peace, freedom, and richness of our true nature when we're still as opposed to feeling frustrations, anxieties, and offenses when using our brains as we go about our lives.

Can we experience the peace, freedom, and richness of our true nature **while** acting in the world? Yes!

My first shift was sudden when for a few weeks I saw only the one benevolent flow. I viscerally got that my previous identity was a mere collection of thoughts. Without these thoughts, the egoic "little me" identity disappeared. My body seemed to be following a natural deep knowing of what to do along with all bodies and all existence as though flowing with a master spontaneous choreography.

Then, the thoughts that structure and evaluate reality returned (thoughts of how I, others, and circumstances "should" be). Any number of seemingly innocuous thoughts could do it:

- "Parents should support their young kids."
- "No one should get my money without my consent."
- "People should be kind."
- "People shouldn't blame me for what isn't my fault."

With these thoughts, a sense of the "little me" returned. I knew the thoughts weren't true, but they still triggered emotions. It was like watching the movies *Gone With the Wind* and *Old Yeller* when I was eight years old--I cried and cried even though my parents assured me they were only movies. Now I wasn't afraid of the thoughts nor fully

2

convinced by them; they had lost their credibility. Still my system responded with intense emotions.

Because I knew that even these thoughts arose from the energy of this single benevolent flow, I curiously investigated them. I wanted to understand the interest from within the single benevolent flow that generated these thoughts. For the next ten years, I constantly investigated my thoughts and emotions, delving deep into their illusion and exploring how they concocted a sense of being a separate vulnerable self.

I embraced the troubling thoughts and emotions like a puzzle to unravel. Intrigued, I discovered the they were often remnants of my conditioning. Holding the thoughts and emotions in spacious awareness, I turned them upside down and teased out their underlying assumptions. I experimented with innumerable types of inquiry, drawing on experience from counseling psychology, spirituality, story-building, etc. I was like an eleven-year-old taking apart a radio to figure out how it works.

Over the years, these twenty techniques emerged because their use revealed wisdom from life's challenging situations and discharged my emotional and physical constriction so that I could directly experience true Being. With consistent practice, I gradually shifted to consistently perceiving the one benevolent flow.

In email exchanges with a friend, I described some of these discoveries and then made my own notes. I'd found how to solve the puzzle and wrote down the solutions! Later many friends noticed the vibrancy and peace in my life and asked what tools I used, and my notes developed into this book.

Chapters three through twenty-two each present life situations and how a particular technique dismantles the assumptions that perpetuate fear and re-establishes the clear perception of the single benevolent flow.

I first shifted perception to the one benevolent flow suddenly, but the abiding experience of it came gradually. Whichever way it occurs for you, these approaches applied consistently can switch you from the old way of perceiving to an awakened way of perception, a perception of the single benevolent flow that you already are.

Awakening is a perceptual shift. Living from the direct experience our true nature, we engage fully and open-heartedly in life because we have nothing to prove, nothing to protect. We recognize that we are life itself. When we think there might be monsters under the bed, we obsess over strategies to keep us safe. Once we know there are no monsters, we freely deal with what is here now and enjoy the flow of life.

How to Read This Book

This book contains almost no information to know, no concepts or ideas worth accumulating. In fact, my disclaimer is that nothing in this book is truth. Instead, it presents a process to stop depending on thoughts to structure our experience of reality. We can intimately experience reality without the layers of concepts and evaluation that we usually add.

For example, when I didn't go to my friend's father's funeral, my friend criticized me saying, "You didn't care," I noticed how I momentarily pulled back. Then, I quickly saw that I was just fine. Her words offended the ideas I held about how I should be perceived. I relaxed back into openness with experience. I listened to her open-heartedly and saw from her perspective. I was intimate with my own falsely-based hurt and then intimate with the her words and tone. I felt compassion without a need to justify or persuade. Then, the response arose in the open-hearted space with lightness rather than judgement, "I love you even though I didn't come to your father's funeral. I apologize that I missed that my attendance was so important to you."

Each chapter includes a summary of the steps of the technique and questions to help you apply the technique, sometimes with additional reflection. As you read, I suggest you place yourself inside the book and compare your experiences to the experiences described. Look to see if the behaviors presented have any similarity to your own behaviors and if the questions apply in some way to your life. Take meditative pauses to see yourself in its pages and allow the reflections to prompt your own reflections. Write your responses to the questions in the spaces provided to cultivate new ways of opening your mind. You may discover that "aha's" are contagious!

As you read the techniques (especially if you read the book more than once), you may start to get a feel for the open mindset that plays with troubling thoughts and disempowers their false certainty. This mindset cultivates curiosity, openness, and freedom in life.

Once you've read through the book and developed a feel for the approach, you may bring a troubling situation to the table of contents and pick a few of the techniques that seem to best match your situation. You can apply the techniques to experiment with new perspectives that feel more aligned with true nature.

Not every technique will match a particular situation you might have, but most situations will match at least a few of the techniques, so feel free to pick and choose techniques and situations that seem to work together.

Dispelling Myths

Bliss, or any other state or emotion, doesn't indicate whether or not we're attuned to the one benevolent flow of reality, neither does getting what we want nor manifesting our dreams. These experiences all may or may not happen.

Once we attune to the one benevolent flow of reality, our identity changes so that we no longer orient according to ideas but instead flow with the fullness of life. Rather than trying to evaluate the river's current from a distance, we are the current itself. The "little me" (separate self) is vulnerable to anxiety, shame, and offense and defined by boundaries and needs. Per the below diagram, a separate identity may be experienced as happy or unhappy, but either way, the determination of happiness is based on particular wants (see the squares). Flowing with the fullness of life feels open, flexible, and without defined limits. We live curiously (see the circle) in infinite wholeness.

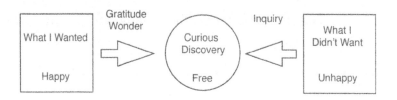

In reality, every moment we are an expression of the unknown, in constant discovery. We are whole and complete even when we imagine otherwise.

Disclaimer

Nothing in this book is truth. These practices helped me and others to drop the thoughts that cause fear, anxiety, shame, and offense and to cultivate an abiding recognition of what we are.

What we are is beyond words. Although it's unchanging, our experience of it can vary from potent nothingness to the current of life emanating all movement, the one benevolent flow. For ease of communication, this book often uses the phrase true Being. In reality, we are always true Being and can never be anything but true Being. Even our imagined "little me" (based in beliefs) occurs within true Being. These techniques undo the habits of mind that imagine the "little me" so that our perception aligns with the reality of our true Being. They decondition our interpretations and assumptions so that during day-to-day life we more directly experience the peace and freedom of what we already are.

All these words seem to indicate that we are deficient or have something to achieve. This is not so but rather a difficulty in using language. In fact, the interest for the exploration arises naturally and irresistibly as part of this projected experience of humanness within the reality of true Being. Our "journey" from where we already are to where we already are (no distance to traverse) is what true Being often projects when it projects a human being. We're merely flowing with life's own movement.

I'm not a teacher. If something here resonates for you, then I'm merely voicing what your inner teacher knows. If it doesn't resonate for you, please turn your attention to whatever does.

1:

Background--An Awakening

The single benevolent flow is complete and full each moment even as it transitions into the next moment. Once my perception shifted to this simple experience, I knew a lightness and fulfillment that no thought-based reality could compare with, free of problems and any danger.

Natural Role of Thoughts

Our thoughts are tools that notice patterns, create models, and use these models to create more tools. Our thoughts cannot, however, create an authentic representation of reality. Nevertheless, most humans go through a stage where we use our thoughts so much that we treat our mental interpretations of reality as though they *are* reality.

As a simple example, we might say we're going to the store to buy the special shears that are exactly right for our project and that we saw there last week. In our mind's eye, we think we know what is going to happen in the next thirty minutes. Now, any number of other things could happen. Our car might not make it to the store, the store may not have what we want, we might get a call to take care of something else that is more urgent, etc. If we believed what we thought in our mind was the optimum reality, then we're likely to be disappointed. Our mental idea and what life brings don't match, and rather than fully being in the experience that comes our way with openness and curiosity, we step back in evaluation. The moment we step back, we lose touch with the fullness of the moment. Our lens of evaluation distances us from the natural nourishment present in reality. And, if we find that we prefer something else, we add struggle and suffering to the moment.

Now, if we'd left for the store wondering what was going to happen, holding the idea of the shears lightly as a possible outcome, we'd have a very different experience. We'd remain in discovery, flexibly shifting as reality directed our steps in each unfolding moment. We'd attend to whatever arose, knowing that reality is always better than an imagined projection. We'd be nourished by the realness of the now, we'd be curious and responsive, and we'd see the grace that underlies each moment of life. There would be no sense of loss because each moment was full of its own unfolding experience.

In normal human development, humans learn to mentally distance from reality into interpretation. And, this step is the origin of suffering, insufficiency, and limitation. At an early age, we create a mental identity of who we are and unconsciously block our intimate experience of the flow of reality. In this stage of mental identification, we don't fully experience the peace and freedom of our infinite Being. However, we can discover new ways of perceiving in which we recognize true Being, the single benevolent flow of life.

Formation of a Thought-Based Identity

I remember the moment at two years old when a pattern of thoughts solidified to make an apparent "Lisa" (a thought-based identity centered around my preferences). Up until then, I'd been in a hazy flow of desires, instincts, and sensory input. However, at this moment, a normal stage in human development, I established a pattern of suffering that persisted for the next thirty-six years.

My next-door neighbors were moving away, and our visit was a short goodbye visit. I wanted to go into the bedroom to play with the daughter like I always did, but my parents wanted us to stay in the living room because the visit was to be short. After a little while, my two-year-old mind decided that my parents had been wrong and that there had been enough time to play in the bedroom. Reflecting on this situation, I decided that my parents didn't always know best; sometimes I might know better. I concluded that I had to look out for my own interests.

With these thoughts came beliefs such as the following:

- I know best how things should go for myself.
- I need to strategize to get what I think is best.
- Life brings obstacles that can prevent me from getting what is best for me.

I didn't know at this young age that these thoughts are common to everyone and that they lie at the core of how we create suffering for ourselves by arguing with life's unfolding as we pit our will against what happens.

By the time I was a young adult, I had settled on my preferred strategies that I believed would help me get what I wanted. I thought that if I were always loving, responsible, and self-sufficient then people and life would cooperate with what I wanted. I had a frequent stream of thoughts that evaluated me against these requirements. And, when I didn't get what I wanted, I quickly pointed to some failure on my part as the cause of the unwanted event, which gave me a sense of control over my world. When I got what I wanted, I believed I'd earned it by living up to my requirements. For example, I applied to many scholarships for college. When I received a scholarship, I took credit based on my hard work. When I didn't receive the scholarship, I thought I must not have worked hard enough. I didn't fully consider that I received the scholarship because of the generosity of the donors or that I didn't receive the scholarship because life was sharing the blessings with others. In my mind I was striving for a limited resource rather than flowing in a current of abundant resources, all of which were shared in the perfect balance of the moment. Because of my lens of interpretation, I perceived life's events as consistent with my strategy of managing life. And, I tended to ignore evidence to the contrary. I also was especially sensitive to criticism that I was less than loving, responsible, and self-sufficient.

Obeying the rules I imposed on myself to help get me what I wanted, per my own beliefs of how life worked, I was under an onerous taskmaster. This taskmaster of life strategies assumed how I should be, how my life should unfold, which school I should get into, which people should like me, how supervisors should perceive me, and so on. Even when I naturally wanted to do something well (by its standards), the taskmaster would add the thought that I *should* do it well, bringing an element of struggle before I even began the task.

As I tried to live life from the perspective of the mental taskmaster, I had a sense of imminent trouble since its strategies focused on narrow outcomes prescribed before seeing how life would unfold. For example, if my work project got cancelled or a relationship ended, my first instinct was anxiety and grief because my plan was for these things to last even if what came next was better than what was before. All of our attempts to control eventually bring disappointment and suffering.

Any time we prefer our plans over what is, whether in ourselves, our circumstances, or other people, we suffer. I discovered this suffering invites us to identify our ideas and strategies, question them, and open to our lives with curiosity and open-hearted engagement. From this place, we discover that life is benign and full. When we live life more fluidly and attuned, we experience natural intimacy and connection.

Shifting from Living in a Thought-Based Reality

During some prominent life moments, I glimpsed ways of living that didn't depend on my strategies and experienced reality's natural benevolence. For example, in the Landmark Forum (a three-day workshop offered globally), I saw that I'd focused a lot of energy on accumulating money because my mental taskmaster believed that money was hard to come by and that its accumulation was a necessary ingredient for my self-sufficiency. In reality, I lived easily on less than I made, but I made my career choices according to this supposed need for money rather than by my enjoyment of my work. I conceived a problem (I needed more money), and I was investing my life in solving that trumped up problem! My belief had turned my life into an uphill climb that was totally unnecessary. I realized that I could change careers and still easily maintain my lifestyle.

Similarly, I believed that marriages should always last until death. To comply with this belief, I tried every approach I knew to make my husband and I stay together. In the moment that I finally opened to reality and granted myself permission to divorce, waves of love for the whole world rolled through me. I felt more open-hearted than ever before. If I wanted to experience love and connection, then I'd been going about it backwards. When we open to reality as it is, we relate more lovingly than when we struggle to obey idealistic (and suffocating) beliefs.

So, how did I shift from struggle to lightness and freedom?

When a friend described enlightenment as being present with reality, something clicked for me even though I couldn't mentally understand what he was describing. Somehow I sensed that he was pointing to an ongoing intimacy with all-that-is, separate from effort and evaluation. I explored various practices and teachers to help me learn to be more present. As I became more open to reality as it is, I felt a deepening connection to the flow of life in me.

Then, I went to a week-long silent retreat with Ady-ashanti. I shared a bathroom with many other women but couldn't verbally communicate with them. Normally, I'd be my "considerate self" and negotiate turns at the sink and so on. In this case, I did the best I could and took a break from the "considerate self." In fact, in silence I couldn't do much towards my standards of being loving, respon-sible, and self-sufficient. My goal was that enlightenment (whatever that was) would happen to me. Then, halfway through the retreat, I realized that I was wasting the re-treat by focusing on something in the future! So, I let go of all goals and just enjoyed following the schedule and rest-ing as simple awareness. I woke up Thursday morning, and the thoughts that created a sense of my identity were gone. I was pure sensing and movement. I saw how my thoughts had always rushed to imagine every potential scenario coming up in my life so that my mind could claim to have made the choices for any of those scenarios. Now all those thoughts had stopped, yet somehow I seemed to know what to do without thinking about it. I saw that my mind had never actually made decisions—decisions had always just come to me. The whole world in fact flowed as a single movement. My mind had made up stories to in-terpret and explain the movement, but the choreography was a simple dance of people coming together and then moving apart. Experiencing the simpleness of reality in this way felt light and free.

For a few weeks, this simplicity of flow persisted. Then, gradually the thoughts that created a sense of a separate identity returned but without their former persuasiveness. I knew this identity did not exist, that it was a result of assumptions and interpretations—all mental constructs. I also knew that even these thoughts were somehow part of the flow. I became fascinated with how thoughts could give an illusion of having a separate identity and wanted to learn all I could from this experience.

Over time I learned to see through the illusion of the separate identity and to return to the lived recognition of a single flow of existence. I discovered how to use struggle and suffering as markers of the ideas and beliefs that created this sense of a separate identity. And, I found numerous ways to unravel these assumptions and interpretations so that I could recognize again the simple flow of reality that is always here.

My mind is no longer governed by ideas of how I or life should be. I welcome any psychological discomfort I experience as a nudge to discover how I'm over doing it.

I have new preferences now—alignment with reality is my priority. For example, when a project (e.g, house remodel) takes longer than I first thought and requires additional professionals or tradesmen, I notice the blessing of reality bringing more people into my life to engage with than I might have planned. I've shifted my values so that I value human interactions more and achieving goals less.

I've found that all events, including the painful disease of my loved one, apparent emotional abuse, extreme pain and near death, or any other challenging circumstances turn out to be misunderstood gifts. It's not me against reality.

I am that which enjoys every experience even when my personality may not.

As an inseparable part of reality, I engage whole-heartedly without resistance and follow the impulses that arise within me toward fullness of life as strands in the fabric of reality. I grow by simply remaining open and paying attention rather than from mental admonitions. Every moment couldn't be better than it already is--reality is fundamentally and generously benevolent. And I am naturally right for each situation that comes my way, a fluid movement of numerous attributes.

From working with life's apparent challenges, I've developed twenty exercises that return me to the lightness, ease, and fullness inherent in all experience. I offer them so that you can experiment with them yourself and find your own discoveries. They are meant to be used, not believed or disbelieved.

Questions:

1. When you feel yourself aligned with life (or reality or truth or whatever you term it), what are some hallmarks that signal this alignment to you? What do you know or experience in those moments? [e.g, heart feels expansive, am gentle with human foibles]

_____

_____

_____

_____

2. What are some mental standards you impose on yourself and your life, expectations that when they aren't met, you feel distressed? [e.g., superiors should be fair and honest, I should have work-life balance]

_____

_____

_____

_____

3. When has life worked out even though it didn't follow your ideas of how your life should be? [boss lied to me but helped avoid needless conflict and led to better job]

_____

_____

_____

_____

2:

Background--True Being and the Source of Suffering

The true essence of me (and you) can never be hurt or harmed. It's the precursor of even energy itself—more a living verb than a definable noun. To live as our true nature, without the fabrication of a separate identity, brings freedom with no need to add anything to ourselves. Awakening can be described as a change from defining ourselves with mental constructs (e.g., the funny intelligent one or the gentle insightful one, etc.) to knowing ourselves as true Being (a fluid expression that can be teacher or student, quiet or loud, giving or receiving, etc.). This chapter will develop this foundation further, and the next chapters will each present a different technique for more fully experiencing our true nature.

How Thought-Based Identities are Constructed

When we believe ourselves to be the mental identity defined by our expectations and evaluations, we live a fragile existence subject to anxiety, shame, and offense, first and foremost because the mental identity doesn't really exist–it's maintained by a system of beliefs that we hold onto and with which we try to get others to agree. Because self-identification through ideation is so instinctive to a human brain, we usually aren't aware we're doing it. Although meditation and many other practices may help relax this habit, the most direct way to help it relax is to investigate each time we feel offended, disappointed, hurt, criticized, misunderstood, threatened, abandoned, controlled, or violated. None of these things can happen to true Being! Only our mentally constructed identity can experience any of these things.

For example, suppose we take the "wrong" route to an event and we're very late and someone says to us, "you're incompetent" (or inconsiderate or negligent, etc.). This sentence is merely words out of their mouth, neither true nor untrue, an expression of their experience that we may or may not consider. No offense occurs unless we're invested in their perception of us as competent (or considerate or responsible, etc.) in which case the idea we want for ourselves has been challenged. Because their words challenge our self-concept, our thought-based identity is offended.

True Being, however, remains unoffended. True Being is beyond words and is indestructible; we might say it's the aware space through which all our experiences pass. Any experience may pass through the space, but the space is not defined by what passes through it just like the sky is not changed by clouds passing through. True Being doesn't argue with or resist what is—not that it is passive either. The conditions of the sky may cause clouds to dissipate or condense as rain. Likewise, as learning and change happens within the space, there is a natural flow of life's impulses that engage with what is. Life's impulses emerge from true Being.

One way to recognize true Being is to feel it as the alive essence that makes the present moment real. Anything in the past or future is held only in our minds and lacks this realness. We teach children the difference between the pretend bear and the real bear, and we can teach ourselves the difference between the past and future versus the present moment. The first two aren't real; only the present moment has the vividness of reality. Our thought-based conceptualization of reality also lacks this realness because it's only a mental construct.

True Being isn't threatened by other people's words and actions and accepts them exactly as they are. Acceptance doesn't mean that true Being happily believes the other person's words. True Being peacefully moves into appropriate action, compassionately supporting or leaving or even making police reports, etc., if so moved, all without taking offense, allowing others the freedom of their own experiences.

For example, if we believe, "others should respect my opinion," (e.g., at a project planning meeting or during a big purchase) then we notice when people respect our opinion and when they don't, and we go into fight or flight when people are too out of line with our expectations. Our assessment of their level of respect determines how we evaluate them and guides our reactions. This mental construct frames our experience and our behavior as we internally crusade for our cause. Our mental ideations set us up as judges over life, always keeping a tally.

Not only does offense indicate our thought-based identity at play, but effort and control indicate our thought-based identity at play. For example, we may arrive to the event in plenty of time with all our responsibilities filled to the T. If there is a strong sense of personal coordination and achievement, we're also operating from a thought-based identity. In this case we may be very sophisticated, seeming to get many things in life to operate as we want them to, thinking we're free when in fact we're taking excessive credit. We don't recognize our care and watch-fulness until something veers from our plan.

In contrast, as true Being, we're fluid in each unique circumstance; our peace doesn't depend on things follow-ing the plan. We live from curiosity and wonder regardless of whether plans line up or not. For example, in conversa-tions we tend to be open to the whole group rather than dominated by our own agenda. We flex our plans as peo-ple offer input and co-create together. We leave conver-sations more interested in what was created by the whole rather than in how our objectives were achieved.

At this point, a common objection is that if someone attacks my body, say they cut off my hand, then that must be considered a true attack. My response is that my body has been attacked. My body no longer has one of its hands. True Being, however, remains unchanged. Of course, I naturally want to take care of my body, and I respond accordingly. My severed hand is a new situation to deal with. Grounded in true Being, I'll have the most collected frame of mind to respond quickly, proactively, and effectively. If I'm troubled by ideations of the disaster this means for the rest of my life, my mental anguish and panic will likely make a difficult situation into a catastro-phe. My body can be attacked, but true Being can't be attacked. Acting from this knowing is the best possible option for handling the physical attack.

It may seem that even true Being suffers in extreme situations, but I haven't found a single example, and I've tested it pretty thoroughly. Even in extreme physical pain, I've discovered that I become absolutely present, living through each moment. My body may be hurting terrifically, but if my mind doesn't argue or project further problems, I come into a still point of one moment with pain and then another moment with pain. I am true Being, the still aware space living around and through the physical pain. True Being's inherent equanimity is steadfast.

So, when we're offended or disappointed, it's something in our ideas about how we should be or how life should be that has been affronted—not true Being. When I suffer, I've invested myself in ideas that don't line up with reality. Thought-based identities are easily offended by mere words since they exist in the realm of words and beliefs.

Identifying the Self-Concepts Causing the Perception of Separation

Because our thought-based identities are habitual ideations, trying to recognize them is like trying to see a perfectly camouflaged walking stick insect in a pile of twigs. Our thought-based identities are, for the most part, similarly undetectable. Now, suppose that walking stick insect moves; then we can find it by its motion. In a similar way, we can spot our thought-based identities when we see that we're feeling offended, threatened, or put down.

So, our experiences of offense or threat are invaluable as they help us recognize the ideas we've invested in that conflict with reality. These ideas are often completely innocuous except that they paint us and reality into a box (e.g., I don't hurt people, everyone should get the same chance, everyone should keep their commitments, etc.). As we prioritize knowing true Being, then each moment of supposed "offense" becomes a tremendous gift–the "hurt" points out our otherwise hidden assumptions beneath our thought-based identities. Once I define the conflicting belief or assumption, then I inquire (e.g., via the techniques in the books) to dismantle the relevant thoughts in my thought-based identity and find myself liberated from those particular thoughts. I become free to respond in any way appropriate because I'm no longer trying to prove anything.

The single benevolent flow is not a sanitized version of our favorite ideals. It's an infinite kaleidoscope of giving and receiving, rushing and stillness, noise and silence, being big and being small. As we recognize that Being permeates and persists through it all, fear is replaced by curiosity, and wariness is replaced by freedom.

So often our own beliefs limit us more than the situation itself! For example, our boss asks us to take on an extra project when it simply doesn't work for us. We may think our boss is demanding, but it's our own belief that we should obey our boss that is demanding. Once we have no belief to live up to, we can kindly tell our boss what works for us and negotiate a solution. We might even take on the request with the warning that other projects may run late. His ongoing complaints or demands bear less weight when we don't have the belief that our boss should always be pleased with us. As a second example, suppose the flow of life calls for something that feels limiting to our small identity (e.g., a job that seems like a poor fit). Without our beliefs, we do what is before us and rest as true Being, touching into the fullness of life that is always vibrant and full. Without the beliefs of what type of job fits us, there is no problem.

When we aren't operating from our thought-based identities, we relax naturally into true Being, experiencing completeness and lightness.

So, to summarize, the overall approach underlying every technique is

---

1. **Notice when you feel hurt (offended, threatened, etc.).**
2. **Identify what you think should be instead.**
3. **Choose a technique from this book to unravel your thinking.**

We're already and always true Being–it's merely our ideas that prevent us from living in this recognition.

Most of the "should-be" ideas that cause us suffering seem so true that it would never even cross our minds to question them. To question our assumptions and beliefs takes an open mind and a willing heart.

Many versions of questioning our thoughts are taught and overlap with one another. The most thorough process I've found is taught at thework.com by Byron Katie (which is presented as the final technique in this book).

What makes the biggest difference in the impact of any questioning is *how* it is practiced. Habitual thoughts don't exist in our heads; they're integrated in our emotions, in the stances we take in life, and in how relate. So, questioning has to go deep enough to include all of our experience so that the conditioning itself shifts rather than just the concepts in our heads. I demonstrate this more integrated approach in each of the techniques.

An Experiment Not a Concept

I'm not asking you to believe that separation and suffering is caused by our own beliefs about how things should be. I'm offering that if you try these experiments that help relax our beliefs about how things should be, you'll find that suffering is reduced in your life and you'll experience more freedom. With regular use of these exercises, you'll live less from a thought-based identity and experience yourself more as one with the benevolent flow of life.

As an example, I had a technician job that seemed to use less than my full potential. When I believed that "I'm intelligent and creative and my job should exhibit these abilities," I'd tell people what my job was and then list my academic degrees. I was covering over a sense of inadequacy about my job at the time. When I was at work doing my job, however, I'd often get happily lost in the flow of my work, meeting interesting people, using interesting equipment, rushing to meet a deadline, or pausing to enjoy a break when things were slow. Nothing was wrong about my job until I believed the idea that I should use my abilities to their full potential. I noticed this twinge of embarrassment at various moments and knew it was a sign that I unconsciously believed something that conflicted with reality—a perfect opportunity to let go of another "should-be" idea in my quest to live from true Being. In this case I identified the belief that my job should exhibit my abilities and then sat meditatively and relaxed fully until I felt myself immersed in and saturated with true Being. I wanted to see this situation from the perspective of true Being. I tuned in more and more deeply, feeling true Being as full, timeless, and absolutely complete. Almost like savoring a fine wine, I savored the full completeness of true Being for many minutes. As I immersed myself in this experience, it became clear to me that no doing or activity of mine could add to the perfection of true Being. I recognized at the deepest level that true Being is what I am and that true Being is the source of all meaning and value. As an expression of true Being, I'm full to overflowing with completeness–anything I do is at most an extra curiosity that can never add or diminish this inherent value. Grounded in this knowing, I've found myself living my life unconcerned about whether my job or any actions demonstrate my abilities. I have no need to prove to anyone that I'm intelligent or creative, etc., and am not embarrassed or concerned about how I'm perceived.

As I've questioned painful beliefs until they fall away, I've found myself living in a continuous flow of sensations, many pleasurable, all interesting, some moving me into action and some with physical pain. No suffering exists. Suffering happens when I add hurtful meanings to situations. Even physical pain is minimized when I don't cogitate about it–my anticipation and rehearsing of pain and focusing on how it limits what I can do greatly exacerbate it, converting it to suffering.

Without my ideas of how things should be, I experience the universe as inherently supportive. Life expressing in each part (person, circumstance, etc.) is a single force, weaving one unfolding fabric.

Some might think that to flow with life would be a passive existence. On the contrary, my engaged responses flow freely as a part of the whole evolving harmony. I enjoy the present as perfect and enjoy impulses toward what is next as a natural ongoing flow. My acceptance frees me from constant second-guessing and from attachment to the outcome. I simply respond as life calls.

Experiencing True Being

What does it feel like to flow as true Being? You can try this exercise: tune into the part of you that has never changed. Sense what you are beneath all thoughts, feelings, and experiences; sense down to the indivisible, immutable being essence that is aware of everything else. Sinking into this space of awareness, feel its timelessness, its vitality, and its equanimity. Resting as this awareness, allow your consciousness to diffuse through this aware space and notice the absence of any edge or boundary. This essential presence is beyond time and permeates all that is. Being indestructible and omnipresent, it has an essence that is more real than anything else. It's the silence before all sound, the prime mover that generates all movement, the awareness that knows any experience before it is named. It is a vast nothingness from which emanates the basic essence of all being.

Like the bumpers on a bowling lane that prevent the ball from going into the gutter, suffering nudges us back from our unquestioned ideas of how things should be. The sooner we catch ourselves suffering, the sooner we question our thoughts and beliefs until they lose their certainty and dissolve, and we return to freedom, oneness, and peace. Additionally, if we lower our tolerance for suffering, then as soon as we get a whiff of suffering, we can question our beliefs. We then abide in the effortless flow of true Being.

Questions:

1. In what ways do you see yourself or your life as less than you or it should be? [e.g., I didn't learn to stand up for myself]

_____

_____

_____

_____

2. What happens because you believe these ideas? [e.g., I feel impotent]

_____

_____

_____

3. What would happen if you didn't believe those ideas? [Ie.g., I'd like my life and think myself affable]

_____

_____

_____

4. In what ways do you see others in your life as less than they should be? [e.g., my parents should have taught me better, people should listen to me more]

_____

_____

_____

5. What happens because you believe these ideas?
   [e.g., I feel like I'm living my 2nd best life]

_____

_____

_____

6. What would happen if you didn't believe these
   ideas? [e.g., I'd see myself as a considerate person,
   internally strong, who spreads peace and helps
   ground out negative energy by my non-reactivity]

_____

_____

_____

3:

Technique 1 Direct Re-cognition

The first option in dismantling my beliefs and thought-based identity is the most direct but the most challenging technique. I might call it "direct re-cognition."

This technique is to (1) identify a painful assumption and look for a reversed viewpoint, and then (2) open my mind to meditatively discover new interpretations that re-orient my perceptions toward seeing the support in the situation. In this way I disrupt my beliefs and discover peace. To consider the reversed viewpoint is NOT to replace an old belief with a new belief. Rather, to consider the reversed viewpoint is to look at the opposite of my interpretation with an open mind and heart and explore how I might have overlooked some of my experiences that would substantiate this opposite interpretation. Here's an example:

Example: My Mom Loves Me

By the time I was thirty-two, I'd developed boundaries with my mom because over the years she had said things that I interpreted as critical. A Landmark Forum leader (Roger Smith who led the workshop I took in 2004) told me that he knew that my mom loved me very much. "Moms love their kids," he said matter-of-factly with absolute conviction (not as a belief but as a knowing from experience with thousands of moms of every type). I was the one who was withholding love from her, he explained. That blew my mind.

"Moms love their kids." If I were to look in my experience to see if that might be true, I reflected, I'd have to give up being right, consider that my interpretations were based on a limited understanding of the situation, and consider that being treated differently than I preferred didn't matter as much as I thought it did. Contemplating "Moms love their kids," I considered that perhaps I was missing part of the picture. Opening further to these possibilities, I felt an uncomfortable diminishment of my thought-based identity. I could either reaffirm my old interpretations and continue with my boundaries with my mom, *or* I could allow myself to drop the ideas I'd been holding, become less reified around my ideas and try on this new way of thinking.

My teacher gave me a glimpse of a very different way of relating. And a part of me resonated with his way of seeing things. Although I'd have to admit that I'd been wrong, I'd be happier. I wasn't used to prioritizing this part of me (that was more flexible in reading people and less interested in being right), and I almost overlooked it all together, but a small inner impulse toward more openness and less guardedness prompted me to continue down this new path to a broader understanding.

I considered that I'd been wrong all along. Perhaps everything my mom had done and said always included her love for me. Initially, I was so stuck in my interpretations that seeing from this new perspective felt like a puzzle—fortunately, I love puzzles! Using this new premise, I went back to past situations to see how I might perceive them differently. It was a fun challenge, almost a game.

"My mom had always loved me." First I contemplated that thought and looked for evidence. Very quickly I was overwhelmed with the list of all she'd done for me—her care, sacrifice, and investment in me. Looking with no identity to protect, I saw her love in countless details of my life. Her love was clearly ever present, a consideration in all her major choices. Next, I started looking, one by one, at the moments she'd seemed critical; I felt the stirrings of a paradigm shift.

I meditatively opened to new interpretations and saw that some of what I'd considered criticism was merely her advice in an attempt to help me have a good life based on her understanding. She was concerned from time to time that I'd have to face avoidable difficulties. Of course, she loved me; she was thinking about me a lot and hoping to help save me some pain! I continued looking. Other things she said were her attempts to increase our contact. She missed me. Transitioning from a mom who was engaged almost full-time in the care of her children to being the parent of adults was no easy task. In every situation I saw her love and how I'd been pushing her away.

Then came the big aha: I was still trying to prove that I was a "good daughter" by getting her to be happy with me. I was still measuring myself by her approval, which meant I wasn't considering myself an independent adult. In fact, I saw that I was so attached to being a "good daughter" that I turned every interaction with her into a points system—had I earned a "good daughter" point or not?

It was time to let go of my identity as a "good daughter" and my need for my mom's approval. I also decided to give her the freedom to have all her concerns, whatever they were. Her concerns were hers to deal with; they were in no way a diminishment of her love for me. Above it all, she loved me; I loved her. It was as simple as that.

Operating with such freedom for myself and for my mom was unknown territory. At first my habitual thought-based identity with all its interpretations and preferences kept coming back. But, I could see my choice was between entanglement (trying to control her and her concerns) or peace, and I kept choosing peace. I chose to drop my identity's need for external validation and focused on the ever-present love between my mom and me. Over the next years, I opened more to my mom, and she felt more connected to me. We naturally grew into a deep, loving friendship between two adults.

I saw how my old ideas of how a mom should behave weren't even humanly possible—I'd wanted validation and independence simultaneously! And I certainly hadn't had space for her growth process as she faced her own concerns. Fortunately, she is a real person from whom I learn so much as I see her go through various stages and situations of life.

Life graciously strips from us our thought-based identities and assumptions about how life should be. It's only painful if we resist that process instead of recognizing its benevolence. When I stood firmly in the perspective that love pervaded even the areas where life didn't follow my (impossible) preferences, I found freedom.

Through this process I noticed my beliefs about how a person who loved me should act and speak with me.

When people didn't follow these unspoken rules (that seemed validated by society), I felt hurt. Now I see that people who love me can say and do any number of things that don't always comply with my preferences, especially if they're feeling concerned or hurt or exhausted at that moment. Their troubled behavior doesn't mean they don't love me. At worst they're confused, and more likely I'm misunderstanding them. Just like I know the sun is shining even on a cloudy day, similarly, my mom loves me even if my expectations cloud my ability to see it. My mom can't not love me.

(Note: I've come to see that just as I've treated people I love with non-loving actions in moments of pain and confusion, so parents do the same. My hurtful actions didn't mean that I didn't love my friends and family. It simply meant that I was lost in my own hurt and confusion and at times expressed that pain, being unable to access and express my love in that moment. Love, including parental love, may be there even when completely clouded over by inner turmoil.)

Furthermore, I saw that true Being isn't offended or hurt–this essence is eternal and inviolable. What was being hurt was my sense of my rights, my beliefs about what I deserved, and my ideas about what was proof that I was loved (it makes me laugh now to think that I wanted frequent proof that I was loved). Underlying all these beliefs was a blind confidence that I knew what was best for my life.

So, to summarize, this technique is to

---

1. **Identify a painful assumption.**
2. **Look from the perspective that life is fundamentally supportive and rephrase the assumption from this perspective, usually as the opposite of the painful assumption.**
3. **Find specific evidence that supports this opposite as equally true.**
4. **Meditatively open my heart to the experience of this opposite.**

In place of my thought-based identity, I foster willingness to discover the benevolence that is always here. After the event above, I wanted to discover more pathways toward peace.

Questions:

1. Find a painful assumption. For example, where have you felt insufficiently loved? Where have you felt a lack of security? Lack of success / fulfillment? Lack of being seen, or whatever applies to you? [e.g., I didn't recognize my gifts until late in life]

_____

_____

_____

_____

2. (Helpful elaboration) What did you choose to do to protect yourself as a result? What was the cost of that protection? [e.g., I tried to be of cheerful service to others to hide my sense of having nothing valuable to share]

_____

_____

_____

_____

3. Reverse the painful assumption. [e.g., In spite of myself, I developed many good relationships and was unknowingly developing my gifts]

_____

_____

_____

_____

4. (Helpful elaboration) What freedom would you have if you saw your experience as perfectly crafted for you? [e.g, Maybe I was subtly expressing and developing my gifts all along--I didn't need anyone to point them out or cultivate them]

_____

_____

_____

_____

5. Open your heart further to this reversal. What ideas would change in your understanding if you experienced the reversal as completely true? [e.g., I would change "gifts should be cultivated early" to "it's been perfect to slowly develop my gifts unconsciously over time"; I would change "a gifted person has more to share" to "the simple person is equally true Being"]

_____

_____

_____

_____

6. (Helpful elaboration) If you let go of being the authority of what was best for you, how would that affect your thought-based identity? [e.g., I'd be light-hearted and appreciative of everyone in my life, whether or not I was gifted]

_____

_____

_____

_____

7. Is freedom and true fulfillment worth experimenting with the new understanding that benevolence has ordered it all? [e.g., yes! I see that life's timing has taught me much more than my timing would have taught me; there's so much more wisdom this way]

_____

_____

_____

_____

4:

Technique 2 Discovering a Personal Broken Record

The thoughts that put a veil between us and the flow of true Being may give themselves away by the repetitiveness of their critiques.

True Being expresses itself in an infinite number of ways (light, serious, strong, tender, boisterous, sensitive, etc.). Our thought-based identity has a much more restricted range. In fact, a few repeating thoughts will frequently assert themselves over and over to give us the feeling tone of our personal identity. Although the assortment of thoughts is remarkably similar across all humanity, each of our thought-based identities tends to have its own preferred subset. This beliefs in this subset become so habitual that they seem to dig a rut into our thinking pathways.

The mere repetitiveness makes the thoughts suspect if we look at them more closely. If an answering service always said, "Good morning," regardless of the actual time of day, we'd question its authenticity; likewise, we learn to question thoughts whose theme and tenor repeat themselves irrespective of changing situations. When we sit in silence and focus simply on the pulse of life coursing in our being, we may notice that many of our thoughts follow a consistent theme. Here's an example.

Example: "I Should Be More Loving and Productive"

Once I'd begun a practice of resting as awareness (one of my preferred meditations), I noticed how my mind easily wandered. Thoughts seemed to come from every direction about any number of topics, and I'd simply bring myself back to the living vibrancy in my body. Over time I became more aware of the observing happening outside of my thoughts and noticed recurrent themes in my thoughts.

Then a friend told me what he'd been distracted by while meditating: memories of people being unkind to him. My automatic internal response was, "Why think of past painful things like that? What's useful about that?" And a light bulb went off! His particular pattern of thoughts wasn't frequent in my own repertoire. Those thoughts seemed useless to me in contrast to my own recurring thoughts of how I'd been unkind to others! I believed rehearsing my failings would somehow make me a better person in the future. However, if his thoughts were so obviously a waste of time to my thinking, I had to consider that maybe my thoughts were an equal waste of time.

I examined my thought patterns more methodically and saw that approximately 90% of my thought patterns generally fell into two categories: rebuking thoughts recalling times I "should've" been kinder or future-oriented thoughts about things I needed to get done.

I was convinced of the value of these thoughts until I saw so clearly the uselessness of my friend's thoughts. Then I saw a broken record aspect to my thoughts. Back when we used nylon records, we recognized a "broken" or scratched record because it kept getting stuck in the same groove and repeating itself endlessly. In the same way, the themes of my thoughts didn't change irrespective of the variety of my life situations. These same recurring thought patterns persisted not only during meditations but also throughout the day.

Now these repetitious thoughts couldn't trick me so easily into believing them. They were just the same message running over and over. This pattern lacked discernment about the uniqueness of any given situation; it had no attunement or true wisdom. Instead, it slapped the same solution with minor variations onto every obstacle in my day! Its cure-all snake oil was "to make life work better I should be more loving and productive." Any time I perceived a problem, my mind could almost always find fault with how I'd treated another person or hadn't done enough, pointing to these failings as the source of the problem. For example, if I got a late fee on a bill, it was because I hadn't been productive enough. (I had to blame something--it couldn't simply be.) If my teammate didn't deliver her part of the project on time, it was because I hadn't been loving and appreciative enough to gain her favor.

These habitual thoughts reified my thought-based identity and were aligned with its themes—that I should be a loving, responsible, self-sufficient person. They rigidly asserted how I knew better how life should go and how I could exert control. I could feel how my body would stiffen with these thoughts, and my heart would feel smaller, my eyes narrower, and my gut tighter.

Wisdom, on the other hand, explores situations with more curiosity and openness, discovering the unseen blessings and flexibly engaging with appreciation. When I meditated, to sit in such openness for extended periods of time challenged my thought-based identity. So, my mind rehearsed past situations that supported my identity that I should be loving and productive to keep hold of my thought-based identity.

The more I inquired into this rehearsal of how I should be loving, the more I saw it as a kingpin to how I perceived and evaluated reality. That I should be loving was a deeply ingrained idea that seemed patently true. This thinking didn't recognize that love might come naturally through me and that love might express itself in unexpected ways. To defy my beliefs about how I should be loving seemed to put me at risk of inevitable isolation and danger. I had a bookkeeper in my head constantly calculating whether or not I'd been loving enough to earn the goodwill I needed to be safe in the world.

As I relaxed this demand to be loving and tested out more flexible ways of responding in life, I let myself act more from whatever kindness was natural (for example, saying no to requests for help). I didn't check to make sure that other people perceived me any particular way. I left situations more open-ended, watching to see how things would turn out without my heavy-handed management. I also noticed my subconscious fears surfacing—fears of disapproval and unpredictable harm and even death.

Finally came a big turning point: after years of giving supreme authority to the internal bookkeeper, I surrendered my position as the authority on whether or not I was loving enough to merit respect among others and a good life (or life at all). I turned over such matters to the universe. I could no longer serve my thought-based standards. I'd keep myself available, open and willing to what naturally wanted to come through me and stop the incessant evaluation against my mental expectations. My mental standards didn't know best. Life knows best. Period. I'm not in control of my existence, my reputation, or my future. I'll live or I won't, end of story. The surrender was huge as I let go of my supposed control, and the relief was even more immense.

Now when I have thoughts that I should be more loving or more productive (e.g., "You should've stayed late to help your co-worker"), I know they're signals of my thought-based identity at work. These mental demands are immediately suspect simply by their very nature. These thoughts are red flags of fabrication. In fact, they've nearly disappeared over the years.

Identifying one's own broken-record thought patterns greatly weakens the thought-based identity. By recognizing the ineptness and burden of these endlessly cycling thoughts, we return more easily to true Being. Each time we notice them, these repetitious thoughts lose their ability to mislead us and instead become reminders to return to true Being.

There are many possible types of broken-record thought patterns, and our own will seem very convincing to us. Some examples are:

1. Things would be better if I had more support.
2. Just keep it fun.
3. Be responsible and uphold good values.
4. I should be prepared.
5. I can figure it out on my own.
6. I get things done.
7. No one understands me.
8. I'm tough—no obstacle is too big for me.
9. No need to get worked up—life should be smooth.

These thoughts are not "bad" thoughts. It's simply that we lose our flexible attunement with the flow of life when we structure our interpretation of reality and our own identity according to these thoughts. They become the stance we have in life and our default position in interacting with others.

Our thought-based identity has no physical reality. It's upheld by a conglomeration of ideas and beliefs that exist only in our thinking. Holding this thought-based identity in place requires a constant effort of reinforcing thoughts. Without our belief in these repetitious thoughts, we become more free, available, and attuned to the flow of life.

This technique is as follows:

---

1. **Pay attention to your thoughts and notice the recurring patterns.**
2. **Summarize the key repeating message(s); these thoughts are the crux of your thought-based identity.**
3. **Surrender the validity of these thoughts.**
4. **Notice these thoughts as they recur, recognizing their underlying purpose to support a mental identity, and question their wisdom.**

Whatever one's particular thought-based identity is, it's fragile and static in contrast to the dynamic and responsive nature of true Being. Life situations call for a much broader range of responses than our thought-based identities are capable of. Life calls in turn for leading and following, changing and holding steady, waiting and acting, strength and tenderness. As an example of our limiting identities, we can all think of the friend we call when we want sympathy and the other friend we call when we want to celebrate. Without our thought-based identity, we access true Being's full repertoire of responses that accord with life's dynamism.

Questions:

1. What are the themes of your recurring thought patterns? [e.g., how other people are unreliable and hypocritical]

_____

_____

_____

_____

2. How might these types of thoughts help assert your identity as independent from the flow of life? [e.g., they make me feel like I have some authority over how things should go]

_____

_____

_____

_____

3. Do your thoughts provide a sense of knowing better how life situations or you or others should be? Do they try to control or protect in some way? [e.g., I feel temporarily stronger because I think I know best and have the right to feel superior]

---

4. What authority or opinions would you have to give up to trust that you and life circumstances are good as they are? [e.g., to accept that everyone is good behaving just as they behave, I'd feel like chaos ruled and nothing had my back; and then to think that this chaos is actually good, I'd have to trust that I don't really know what's best and that floating along in some uncertainty is okay. Funnily, I actually enjoy life more when I do that!]

---

5. What freedom would become available to you if these concerns were no longer yours to manage? [e.g., I'd quit obsessing about others' and my own safety and ride the ups and downs of life without needing extra reassurances; I'd take a wait-and-see approach and just enjoy myself; like the serenity prayer, I'd address what I can change and accept what I cant]

5:

Technique 3 Inner Parts Work

Regardless of how much I've been loved, I've painful-ly interpreted some situations, and I internalized the pain into my thinking and emotions. All of the exercises shared in this book have helped unravel these negative internalizations for me. But, sometimes the pain has been harder to budge. This next technique has been a great comfort to me as it's brought love to areas that felt very unloved. Once I've used this technique several times for a particular situation, it becomes easier to finish the pro-cess with other techniques.

Example: Inner Child Afraid of Making Mistakes

I'll start with an example. For years I wouldn't tolerate some mistakes I made, even coming to tears with shame at work and, looking back, at school and at extracurricular activities through my youth. I criticized myself and need-ed validation through good performance feedback, and couldn't get a handle on this mindset. So, I went through the following process:

1. I looked back to one of the earliest occurrences I could remember. I remember crying in kindergar-ten over my mistakes. I recalled the pain I experi-enced. In this case, I remembered feeling ashamed of my mistakes in an assignment and then scolding myself.

2. Emotionally touching back in to that little girl again, I brought to memory my hurt and frustration. I al-lowed myself to embody this young self and to experience and explore these emotions. I noticed how tired I was of my mistakes, how inferior I felt, and how sometimes I just wanted to die.

3. Next I took the position of the "wise, nurturing adult or parent," my mature self. This mature self re-sponded with compassion and love, assuring the little girl that I understood how she felt and that it was okay to have all those feelings. I asked if she had anything more to share.

4. Taking the position of the little girl, I said that the adult still made mistakes and really wasn't much better. She (the little girl) still felt entirely helpless.

She also shared how she'd felt criticized by others and that criticism had been very painful.

5. Taking the position of the wise, nurturing adult, I honored the little girl for coping so well. I affirmed that she'd been afraid of criticism and had taken this attitude toward mistakes to help herself avoid criticism. I validated that she'd ingeniously used the skills she had at the time and had come up with this self-shaming approach to avoid worse criticism from others. I asked her if she was tired of working so hard.

6. Taking the position of the little girl, I appreciated the acknowledgement and agreed that all this mistake-monitoring was exhausting.

7. Taking the position of the wise, nurturing adult, I said, "Thank you for all your work! I want to relieve you of doing so much. I have new skills of making mistakes and then working through them so that everything works out. I'm still learning, but I can take over now. Are you willing to relax a bit?"

8. Taking the position of the little girt, I agreed to try an experiment of not insisting so much that I couldn't make so many mistakes.

9. Taking the position of the wise, nurturing adult, I offered her a hug.

10. Then I opened into still, present awareness. I let the gentle fullness caress and saturate the wise, nurturing adult, the little girl, all the hurts, and the painful self-shaming. I felt in my body where the shame was especially tight as a grip around my heart. For several minutes I continued to bathe it all with still, present awareness. Emotions washed over and through me. There was no resistance. Memories came up, and I allowed them to rise and subside in turn in their own timing, holding them in love. Eventually there was a profound peace. I welcomed the natural love that expanded through me.

My habit of shaming myself for mistakes was so ingrained that it took many sessions to bring love to all the nooks and crannies of hurt and disappointment. With time something shifted. Mistakes came with only a momentary constricting and then a willingness to move toward acceptance. (Sometimes I no longer saw them as mistakes!) I then questioned the apparent mistakes to see how they were opportunities in disguise, opportunities to ask for help, to humbly recognize others' skills, and to watch how life works things out beyond my control and planning.

The main purpose of this exercise is to bring love and support to an area that is particularly deep and seemingly immovable. Additionally, as we tap into love flowing through us to the hurt parts, we access our true Being.

In fact, one of the greatest joys of human existence is to be an open channel of love, and sometimes this love is channeled inwardly. Regardless of whether we're loving someone outside ourselves or our own inner child, we're the vehicle of true Being as love restores us to our inherent wholeness.

The steps of the practice are to:

---

1. **Identify an early moment of the type of hurt you want to address.**

2. **Put yourself emotionally into the position of the younger you who had the experience and share how you feel either aloud or on paper.**

3. **Put yourself into the position of the wise, nurturing adult and acknowledge the younger you with appreciation, curiosity, and love.**

4. **Put yourself into the position of the younger you and detail further what hurt you experienced and what you need now.**

5. **Put yourself in the position of the wise, nurturing adult and specifically appreciate how the younger you coped as well as she or he did and affirm your love for the younger you. Offer that maybe it has been a lot of work to carry such a burden over the years.**

6. Put yourself in the position of the younger you and express how you feel in response to the acknowledgement and love.

7. Taking the position of the wise, nurturing adult, offer your adult skills to take over the burden carried by the younger you. Commit to making this a focus of ongoing growth and development.

8. Taking the position of the younger you, see if you can find any willingness to let go of at least some of the burden and trust it to the wise, nurturing you.

9. Taking the position of the wise, nurturing adult, offer the younger you your love, perhaps in the form of a hug.

10. Open your whole being to still present awareness. Allow its gentle fullness to hold all the parts, all the memories, all the emotions. Feel into your body and notice the sensations. Without controlling, let it all come and go of its own accord, staying grounded in the still present awareness throughout the process. Notice the final peace or love that remains.

It may feel awkward at first to identify separate parts within oneself, but practice brings greater ease. The boundless love and holding available in true Being is beyond comprehension. Its tender understanding and acceptance can't be overestimated. As we access our own wise, nurturing selves, we start to break down the walls that otherwise try to control this love. The tenderness of this practice gently brings nourishing love and support to deep-seated hurts.

Questions:

1. If you have one, identify a particular area of hurt that has remained hidden or unmoved through the years. [e.g., I felt like my parents lives would be better if I hadn't been born.]

_____

_____

_____

_____

2. Ask yourself if you're willing to have some opening in this area. If the answer is no, find another area. If the answer is yes, proceed to do all ten steps outlined above. [e.g., yes, I'm willing. (1) Child: I feel the little girl who considers herself a burden. (2) Child: I feel so sad and desperate to be different. (3) Adult: I acknowledge the pain of being a burden. (4) Child: I feel angry and helpless that everything I try still leaves me at fault for being needy and in the way. (5) Adult: I understand this sense of helplessness and grief and suggest maybe I've had enough time believing that I'm a burden. (6) Child: That would be too good to be true; I see my parents and other people and no one really seems able to understand or support me like I really need. (7) Adult: I assure myself that my life is doing pretty good. Maybe I don't need that understanding and support; and maybe my parents handled the burden well enough after all. (8) Child: It feels like walking on thin ice, but maybe my parents struggles have been okay for them; and yes, my life is mostly good even without the support I'd like. (9) Adult: I offer to focus on cultivating friendships that are supportive, to take time to listen to my little girl when she feels needy, and to remind us that other people's struggles don't necessarily mean I did

something wrong. (10) I feel lighter and more loving and loved. I then rest in this warmth for several minutes.

Child:

_____

_____

Child:

_____

_____

Adult:

_____

_____

Child:

_____

_____

Adult:

_____

_____

Child:

_____

_____

Adult:

_____

_____

Child:

_____

_____

Adult:

_____

_____

Sensation:

_____

_____

3. How did the loving support and holding change any aspects of your area of hurt? [e.g., I feel like maybe I wasn't so much of a burden and maybe being a burden isn't always a bad thing--just a part of life.]

_____

_____

_____

_____

6:

Technique 4 Bathe in Safety

What is the most safe, protected, nurturing place or situation you can imagine? How would it feel to be so completely safe forever? Now multiply that experience by a hundred. You'd be absolutely safe—not a single thing or person to fear. This safety is how threat-free true Being really is. When I sense beyond my thoughts, emotions, and body to the ground of what is always there, I tune into the essence of Being. It's absolute, unchanging, vibrant, and indestructible. Its fearlessness is so complete that there is no vague caution to temper its curiosity. It's as though its interest propels it to emanate the world of form like pure play with nothing to lose. Relaxing into this depth of indestructible wholeness, I bask in the fullness and timelessness of what we are.

After basking in the safety of true Being, I look at my life and see what needless machinations I put myself through to try to make myself feel safe (as separate from simply taking care of what there is before me to do). For example, I fretted for hours over the email I had to send to my boss because I thought it would displease him when I could've written something simple and direct in thirty minutes or less. My machinations are completely unnecessary. We're safe beyond our wildest dreams. In fact, looking back, I see situation after situation where I feared calamity, and in every situation it worked out as I took each next step. Sometimes I delayed taking the next step because of my anxiety, and then the suffering mounted until I eventually did what was before me to be done. And even in those moments, help came my way!

Support persists at every turn, not always how I expected, but there nonetheless. Support bathes me in ways I don't even notice. School teachers cared about me, employers paid for education, internet articles helped identify health problems, car accidents left me essentially unhurt, friends showed me my self-illusions, monetary loans and gifts got me through tight periods, kind people picked me up when I fell, interests propelled me to enjoyable work, etc. Help has repeatedly turned up when I needed it. People have been patient with me over and over.

Deeper than these supportive situations, timeless and indestructible true Being is the engine of my life. Its vast spaciousness surrounds, envelops, and saturates all experience while itself remaining unperturbed. The knowing Being inside me never ends. It knows how much saliva is in my mouth. It knows where my elbow is even when I'm not paying attention. It knows if I'm breathing in or out when I'm not giving it a thought. This living essence never wavers. Regardless of what happens to my body, I know that true Being continues.

By simply stopping and resting as awareness, we tune into this steady inner Being and are nourished as we sense its potency and equanimity. It's never far because it's what we are. Attuned to true Being, we experience complete safety.

When I spend thirty or sixty minutes marinating in the absolute safety of true Being, I find I have a new perspective on my life. I see how my confused perspectives cause suffering. In that observation, my painful interpretations crumble, and I recognize the caring flow of my life events. Gratitude replaces concern.

Example: Art Promotion Job That Wasn't My Thing

As an example, for two years I worked as an art promoter. I was passionate about the art, which was the work of my best friend who'd died, but I wasn't passionate about art promoting. Some aspects appealed to me, like having the works professionally photographed. Other parts, like soliciting galleries and moving and transporting huge heavy boxes in all kinds of weather, weren't fun. There were moments when I felt out of sync with what was before me and lost on some side path of my true calling. I questioned if I was too timid to venture into whatever would've been a better fit. I envied people who seemed to have better alignment with their work and were doing what they loved.

At the same time, it was clear that this work was the best option for this period. It financially supported me while I trained for another career that seemed more aligned; I had flexible hours and used my spare time for creative outlets. I learned a lot from working with the estate trustee, and I interacted with a lot of people, having invaluable mini exchanges of support, insight, and connection.

Looking back I see even more blessings. Not only did that period support me through a transition, but the trustee had a very hands-off management style that taught me so much. At first when I didn't get responses to emails or didn't get paid in a timely manner, I thought he didn't value my work. Eventually I realized that he so valued my skills that he trusted me implicitly and saw me as highly capable and as someone who didn't need guidance. Now I've worked for another similar manager in work that I love, and our relationship has flowed easily because I appreciate such a hands-off approach. Life supports me every step of the way.

From a position of fear, I interpreted my work for those years as out-of-sync, a crutch at best--life had apparently abandoned me, and I was left struggling. When I opened to the profound safety of true Being, my perspective changed. Without fear as my framework, I saw a flow of support, full of unexpected blessings.

In fact, from a framework of support and sufficiency, I no longer saw a *need* for me to be or do anything more than I was being or doing. I was "chopping wood and carrying water" (a Buddhist concept that the extraordinary permeates the ordinary). I was learning and growing from every new interaction. I inspired others via multiple art shows (the art was very exuberant and life-affirming). I flowed with life day by day with all my needs met. Life was play if I just noticed.

When I open my mind and heart and tune into the profound safety of true Being, I see that when I feel less than supported, in reality I'm surrounded by support. The flow of my life doesn't follow any conventional recipe for success, but it's been an amazing choreography of supportive encounters and deepening into true Being.

To know this infinite support doesn't mean I don't take action to take care of myself. On the contrary, I see my energy and abilities and opportunities to work as gifts from life that provide me support. I'm not a passive receiver—my own body and mind are part of this flow through which

I have what I need. As I pay attention, I discover there is no task too small or mundane to be a vehicle of grace.

The steps of this practice are to

---

1. **Imagine being absolutely safe and protected and sense into that.**

2. **Imagine being 100 times that safe and protected and sense into that.**

3. **Staying in that experience, notice a problem or dilemma in life.**

4. **Meditatively contemplate the following: How are my own fixations aggravating the situation? Is there another interpretation I'd have if I saw the situation as occurring within a flow of safety and benevolence?**

5. **If you open to not knowing, is there really a problem?**

Questions:

1. Where do you feel out on a limb? [e.g., my teen-
   ager isn't telling me what's going on in his life and
   stays in his room]

_____

_____

_____

2. Take thirty minutes to rest as awareness (that is,
   move past thoughts and emotions and notice life
   pulsing through your body, notice what is aware of
   everything else and feel its aliveness, notice what
   is aware of your left elbow even when you can't
   see it, notice what is aware of your right big toe,
   rest as this awareness and relax in the absolute
   indestructibility of true Being). Then, consider that
   life is wholly orchestrated for your ultimate well-being and that of everyone you love.

_____

_____

_____

3. Now look at where you feel out on a limb. How is support showing up? What positive things are already present in that experience? [e.g., my son mentioned a teacher at school that he likes, he sleeps here and eats meals with us, I know he's a good kid; I'm just uncomfortable with change but he needs to find his way into adulthood himself. I did it and he can do it too.]

_____

_____

_____

4. If you open to not knowing, is there really a problem? [e.g., my son actually seems to be doing pretty well. I don't know his exact process, and this mystery is a natural part of this stage of life and a good reminder for me to let go]

_____

_____

_____

7:

Technique 5 Discover the Part that Wants this Moment

Without our judgments and classifications, we touch into the preciousness of each moment. Our will aligns with whatever happens, seeing it as right in this moment even while we may take action toward a next step of change. We ask what we can do from here, appreciating what is without making it wrong. Taking a shower is perfect example: we want to be wet, then we want to be dry, flowing from one to the other. We don't make it wrong that we need a shower nor do we make it wrong that we need to be dried; all is part of the process. Likewise all of life is a natural progression. Our actions are part of the flow arising organically as part of the all-that-is and contributing to whatever is its ongoing development.

As we've discussed, our habitual thought patterns demean what is by finding it lacking in some way. As a result, we create a sense of a separate evaluator that is distinct from the universal flow, a thought-based autonomous person who knows better. Nevertheless, at the level of true Being we are still in alignment. One way to shift our focus back to true Being, therefore, is to discover the part of us that wants this moment to be just as it is and values and cherishes our present-moment experience.

To tune into this aspect of ourselves is NOT a mental exercise; rather it's a curious open-hearted meditation that enables us to feel into a part of ourselves that we may not typically access and that we may not understand very well.

Example: Boyfriend Didn't Pay Back My Loan to Him

Here's a personal example. When a boyfriend and I separated, he wouldn't pay back $6000 that he owed me. To lose $6000 to him seemed unfair to my thought-based identity. It offended my belief that I'm a strong autonomous adult, and I felt used and deceived. I applied this technique of waiting and listening to find out how some part of me might want him not to pay me back the $6000.

Two insights eventually came to my heart. (Many things came to my mind, but they lacked the resonating ring of truth.)

The first insight was that he had three children and was having financial difficulties, so the flow of the moment was bringing money his way to help them. From this perspective, the money wasn't supposed to have been a loan after all. It was a gift to his children. Something inside me enjoyed this idea of giving them money. I could feel an alternate set of values at work in this perspective, a set of values that prioritized care and generosity over my autonomy and rights. Something inside me realigned with true nature in this new understanding; a constricted part opened and came alive. As I willingly shifted to these values, my thought-based identity diminished, and I sensed the bigness of true Being.

Second, I had a strong impression that if the flow of the universe was going to "take" money from me, then perhaps the universe would ensure that I had the means to cover this outflow. With this impression, I felt wonder and curiosity--would it prove true? Within a month a friend gave me a better job, and seven months later, I started a relationship with a man who was very generous with me financially. Life validated the realization as the universe more than replenished the financial outflow. As I sat in stillness with this recognition, my orientation toward money changed. I saw that I'm not in charge of "my" money. The universe would orchestrate its outflow and its inflow.

I'm simply to follow its guidance and operate from the provisions I have.

This inner realization felt novel and light. I knew myself again as one with the whole of existence rather than feeling myself to be an isolated, vulnerable entity, and I shifted away from a view of money that supported a separate sense of self versus a view that reaffirms my oneness with all. I was no longer in the box of my principles, but in the mysterious flow, a flow that is always sufficient for what is needed.

I imagine that many people have spent a few thousand dollars on financial seminars, courses, and therapy to find balance in their attitude toward money. Life gave me my own customized intensive workshop! There could've been no better use for the $6000. I aligned with the part of me that wanted the entire situation to occur as it had.

Through my boyfriend's retention of my $6000, the flow of the universe naturally led me to recognize oneness over my ideas of financial fairness, and this orchestration was better than anything my thoughts could've designed. By uncovering the part of me that wanted things to happen exactly as they did, I aligned more with the values and attributes of true Being (in this case, generosity over justice), and my thought-based identity diminished further.

To speak anthropomorphically (which of course isn't entirely accurate), true Being uses everything just as it is right now for our growth—nothing is wrong right now. As we accept what is, we open to the full learning it offers. We discover acceptance (in contrast to resignation) is not a passive position. In this case, I opened to a new way of perceiving money. I also did not give my boyfriend any further loans. Appreciating the present doesn't mean freezing or perpetuating the present! True Being is a continual flow carrying us to the next movement. Our learning from what is right now informs us as we proactively make whatever changes are called for in the next moment.

Had I merely surrendered the $6000 without fully inquiring into my thoughts about the situation, I might've been left with hidden grudges about men and money. Instead, my heart was open, and I easily entered into a relationship with a financially generous man.

Our thought-based identities argue with reality when it doesn't comply with our ideas of what should be so that we defend our positions and miss growth opportunities and even limit our futures. When we align with true Being, we discover a different set of values at play. Tuning into the part of us that in some way wants this moment, we find our perspectives reorienting.

In summary, this practice is

---

1. **When in a situation you don't like, meditatively open and look for a part of you that wants the situation to be as it is.**
2. **Ground in this part of you as the expression of true Being.**

As we see the positives of the situation and feel the underlying good that resonates with our deepest desires, we more and more embody the values and attributes of true Being.

The resulting learning is not predictable. Sometimes I've learned that I have to say no when it's very uncomfortable for my thought-based identity to say no. Remember, true Being is not a sanitized, insipid version of our egoic preference to look good. True Being is not tame—it's awesome and far beyond our limited expectations.

Questions:

1. Recall a situation where reality fell short based on what you preferred. [e.g., I switched from a credentialed school to a non-credentialed school to better align with my interests and never got credentialed]

_____

_____

_____

_____

2. What are some benefits and / or good outcomes that resulted from that situation? [e.g., the non-credentialed program was pivotal in my life learning and life direction]

_____

_____

_____

_____

3. What did you learn from that situation? [e.g., I deepened in presence and learned some of the techniques in this book]

_____

_____

_____

_____

4. What values were served by the good outcomes or benefits? [e.g., although it wasn't as big a help financially, the spiritual growth was tremendous]

_____

_____

_____

_____

5. Could these values and benefits possibly be equally or more important than what you originally wanted? [e.g., I have enough financially and became much richer spiritually, which has been much more important in regards to what matters in life]

_____

_____

_____

_____

6. Can you attune to the part of you that prioritizes these values? [e.g., yes, true Being is a palpable rich mysterious flow of surprises, way better than simply having a credential and the finances associated with that]

_____

_____

_____

_____

8:

Technique 6 Stepping Down from Self-Judgment

There's another class of suffering where we try to simultaneously take the low position and the high position. We consider ourselves deficient in some way (the low position) but are absolutely certain that we know what would be better (the high position). We consider ourselves an absolute unfailing authority of how we should be (the high position) and then conclude that we aren't good enough (the low position). Thought-based identities aren't logically consistent! We can't be both absolutely right and definitively faulty simultaneously. Here are some examples:

1. A person believes himself (or herself) to be unworthy of a relationship or opportunity or gift, which the universe has brought his way, and either doesn't go for it at all or over-compensates, trying to prove

his worthiness for the opportunity. For example, a man spends hours at the gym to impress his new girlfriend, who really wants time talking and sharing with him.

2. A person feels a relationship, opportunity, or gift is too good to be true and doesn't fully enjoy it because she's anxious about the "too good" thing falling through. She believes she knows best what is possible and not possible and denies life the opportunity to prove otherwise. For example, a woman gets a great position at her job but constantly pesters her manager because she needs constant reassurance that she's doing okay, which lowers her manager's evaluation of her.

3. A person feels a relationship, opportunity, or gift doesn't have a guarantee to last, so he can't enjoy the opportunity because he spends so much energy trying to establish structures that will provide more certainty. He unconsciously believes the universe can't do it quite well enough and that he will make up the difference. For example, a man gets an offer from a friend to share in a new business venture, but his fear makes him spend most of his time on the legal details of the arrangement rather than exploring how their strengths complement

each other for business growth, and the relationship deteriorates.

In any of these situations, the flow of life is clearly benevolent, but we try to play "God," acquiescing to the demands of our anxiety about an imagined negative future outcome. We want more than what is being offered—more guarantees, assurances, or validation. If we surrendered our sense of inadequacy and obsessions about the future, then we'd enjoy the present with wonder and gratitude. Of course open receptivity doesn't mean that we be reckless, but rather that we're available for the truly good gifts that come our way.

Our demands for additional certainty, guarantees, and validation in such scenarios may seem normal, reasonable, and fair, but they separate us from the joy available in the present. These demands are derived from our habits of constant evaluation and our preference for living in explicitly defined structures. When we surrender our constant assessing and our belief in future problems, we open to not knowing and experience the benevolent flow of true Being.

Our exercise is first to turn our attention away from what we think is missing and toward ourselves as the evaluator. We identify specifically how the guarantees that we want are based in our certainty that our anxieties are real. For example, we might notice beliefs such as:

1. I'm not good enough.
2. This opportunity is more than I can handle.
3. This opportunity is too good to last.

Can we absolutely know that our anxiety is true? Notice how sure we are and how we try to play "God" and judge the fit between ourselves and the gift. (Of course, there are situations that are clearly a poor fit, and we move on with a simple no. What I'm referring to are situations that trigger our sense of inadequacy or our anxieties and lead us down a tangent of obsessiveness.)

Next we become willing to surrender our certainty and fully receive the gift, living in the unknown. We learn to sense our fear without buying into it. Initially it might feel terrifying, and we might have to surrender the belief again and again in a steady deconditioning process.

We learn to watch the beliefs as they arise while we move forward without imposing our demands. Like most other practices, we're challenged to live on the edge of the present moment without trying to control it. On this edge, we may not feel comfortable, but we'll certainly feel alive, surrendering into gratitude and trembling with awe simultaneously. We also can love the fearful part of us and comfort that part with reassurances that new behaviors are often uncomfortable and that we can handle the situation one day at a time however it plays out. In this case, our discomfort is a sign of growth.

As an example, perhaps a man has the relationship of his dreams, and he wants her (or him) to marry him to guarantee that it will last, but his partner doesn't want marriage. Then each day is a surrender of his "should-be" idea as he opens himself to enjoying with abandon the love that is given. Or perhaps a woman is offered an executive role that she's always wanted, but she'd expected to have more time to grow into the role and feels unsure. She can take the role, ask for guidance as needed, and live every day in wonder without giving credence to the thought that she is in over her head.

There is a very different feeling in my body when I'm grasping tightly onto what isn't certain. I feel fluttering in my stomach, tightness in my limbs, and a lot of pressure inside. When I open to uncertainty, the fluttering is more gentle and spreads through my whole body, my limbs relax, and my skin feels almost permeable as though my whole body is open and fluid with all that surrounds me. The pressure melts away. I've learned to associate the fluttering (which eventually passes) with surrendering my illusion of control--a good thing!

Example: Ambiguous Offer of Financial Support

When my fiancé and I broke up, he offered to financially support me for a couple years since I'd just started a private coaching practice and wasn't financially self-supporting yet. The terms were vague with no definite monthly amount, and he would be actively dating other women. There were no guarantees. The generosity of the moment was obvious, and I happily accepted. Month by month and then into a couple of years, I saw him fall in and out of love. I didn't know if he'd find "the one" before I had established myself. However, I didn't yield to anxiety or ask for a more specific promise. Instead I remained grateful for what was given, spent prudently, and progressed on my venture. I learned that certainty isn't required for joy or for fully relishing the generosity provided. As it turned out, his generosity endured as long as I needed it.

Each time fear and anxiety arise as we open to receiving a gift, the fear and anxiety remind us that the flow of life is not controllable. Life is calling us out of the box of our thought-defined evaluation into the open unknown. We feel the rush of the intensity of the present moment, and we take one step at a time. We love the fearful part without believing it. Rather than retreating into demands for certainty, we can say to life, "your will be done" and open to its inexplicable gifts.

In summary, this practice is to

---

1. **Identify an area of uncertainty or deficiency.**
2. **Turn your attention back on yourself and identify the expectations you're holding.**
3. **Identify the costs of hoping for control in the situation.**
4. **Identify the gift here already.**
5. **Who or what are you blaming for your discomfort?**
6. **See if you can be willing to enjoy what is given without needing anything extra.**

Questions:

1. What is the greatest area of uncertainty in your life? [e.g., my boyfriend is a very warm affectionate guy with several female friends who are attracted to him and I'm worried I'll lose him]

---

2. What are your expectations in this situation? [e.g., my boyfriend should like me better than any other woman and stay with me]

_____

_____

_____

_____

3. How do you try to control what can't be controlled (that is, doing anything more than the appropriate thing and letting it be)? [e.g., I look for the other women's faults and subtly point them out to my boyfriend and then feel small and more insecure]

_____

_____

_____

_____

4. What is the gift that is present in this situation? [e.g., my boyfriend loves me very much]

_____

_____

_____

_____

5. Do you blame yourself or the gift or anything else for the lack of certainty? [e.g., I blame myself for not being more secure and my boyfriend for his interest in his friends]

_____

_____

_____

_____

6. How might you open more fully to enjoy this gift without over focusing on its lack of certainty? [e.g., I can fully enjoy my relationship right now, knowing that I don't know how long it will last but feeling that I feel bigger when I open to not knowing than when I try to control. In fact, enjoyment without future guarantees is a day-by-day encouragement to stay present, and it holds me in the flow of mystery rather than in my tightly defined will]

_____

_____

_____

_____

9:

Technique 7 Self-Love

When I started learning about the importance of self-love, it seemed a necessary stepping-stone to get to the better stuff. Loving myself, I thought, was a basic chore that I understood had to be done if I wanted to have joy and peace. So I dutifully added the requisite elements. First I started taking better care of my body (exercising, eating better, getting more sleep, etc.). I had more energy and a little more confidence, but nothing much changed. Then I learned that I had to take care of myself in my relationships too. So, I was more deliberate about which relationships I invested in, reconciled with people as needed, and related more authentically. My life felt more supportive, but again nothing much changed. Next I learned that my psychological being was equally important, so I went into counseling, read a lot of books, journaled, found creative expression, and resolved past hurts. Now my life was more interesting and my step a little lighter. But I couldn't say I was more than a better version of what I'd been before. Finally I found the crux of self-love.

When I love myself, there are two irreplaceable components: my inner dialogue is unwaveringly approving, and I cherish every experience, including my inner experience as well as my outer experience, my emotions as well as my circumstances. I initially feared that these components would build a bigger ego, but the exact opposite happened.

Example: Rookie Ultrasound Technologist

For example, when I was a new ultrasound technologist (or new at any skill for that matter), I had a habit of noticing where I could've done better and being disappointed with myself. Now and then I'd do an exam and later realize that I could've added something to bring more clarity. At first, I felt burdened with self-recrimination, and the regret solidified my thought-based identity via my egoic judgments. I hated being less experienced than I wanted to be and at times dreaded doing a particularly difficult exam. I was disappointed in myself and wanted to skip up the learning curve, disliking life as it presented itself in these moments.

Self-love required a shift, and it wasn't easy. Being good at my work seemed important, and my evaluations seemed so true! Clearly, however, I was arguing with life, and I knew that arguing with life is a losing game. I had to investigate and be willing to see another perspective. I admitted that I was a new technologist and that I was learning. In fact, the radiologist, my manager, and the senior techs who were mentoring me had all assumed that I'd be coming up to speed for my first year. It was given that I was in a learning phase. I had to laugh that my mental chatter thought it knew better than the experience of the several senior people surrounding me–they knew there was a learning curve! Noticing that I could do an exam better next time meant that I was moving up the learning curve–that's exactly what learning is! I had imagined my knowing could increase without the uncomfortable learning process. Now I broke out laughing. My inner critic was obviously naive and self-indulgent. I started a new inner dialogue from an open willingness to be with what is. The new dialogue replaced criticism every time it arose and said instead, "Congratulations! You're doing better and better!" There was no ego in my congratulation, rather there was a connection with the flow of life in its many phases, a willingness to be the student and participate in the learning process, and a letting go of my preference for being the expert. I found myself leaving my high position of "knowing better" and trusting the flow of true Being.

Next I opened to cherishing my experience. My ego asked, "What is there to cherish about discovering that

I hadn't done an exam as well as I'd hoped?" Clearly cherishing my learning experience wasn't going to be an ego-building exercise! I looked for where I could be grateful; immediately I thought of the radiologist, my manager, and the senior techs. They all were cheering for me! In my junior position, I was actually receiving a lot of support. I also discovered gratitude for myself—for life flowing through me! Taking on a new career at age forty-seven was courageous and an excellent exercise for my brain, and it had enabled a move to a beautiful area of the country. I also felt grateful for the humbling I was experiencing. Knowing my tendency toward independence and sometimes pride, to be the rookie was a good growth experience for me. It helped me rely on others more and be more vulnerable, rather than overly self-assured. I savored the preciousness of my humanness and delighted in how adorable I was in my struggle to be an expert a mere six months into my job. I also enjoyed stretching myself in advancing my new skills—these experiences were key moments of my life. There was so much to enjoy about being the rookie. I learned to welcome each new exam as the pathway to greater self-love as well as professional expertise, and I came to cherish my junior role.

Self-love doesn't mean we believe our thoughts or even our thought-based identity--it means that we stop resisting them and enjoy them as a passing experience.

We embrace our thoughts and situations (including our emotions) as part of our human experience without judging them. And, we seek to understand and appreciate our experience, opening to the growth available in the situation. To believe our thoughts eventually causes pain; to embrace our thoughts without believing them keeps us in inquiry, open to the unknown, in touch with the dynamic present.

The steps of self-love are to

---

1. **Take care of your body.**
2. **Engage in relationships in ways that nurture yourself and others.**
3. **Be present and understanding with your psychology.**
4. **Wherever there is self-talk, make it loving.**
5. **Embrace all your experiences, internal and external.**

It may be difficult to imagine embracing every experience. But, if you imagine yourself as the grandparent of a young child, you can see how every struggle has an adorable quality to it. Or, you can imagine yourself as someone who has miraculously awakened from a long coma. Now, every human experience is precious. Song writers have written of "sweet sorrow" and of almost every conceivable human experience, lauding the human adventure.

Self-love embraces our humanness in an endlessly nurturing and approving perspective. Self-love trusts the flow of life and invites us to, "Tell me all about it," cherishing every detail of our experience, and then gently responds, "Yes, of course, how else could you be?" Self-love resides in the equanimity of true Being, spaciously unperturbed as it notices the preciousness of each new situation, new emotion, and new challenge. It peacefully sees us through to gracious appreciation.

Questions:

1. Can you find a willingness to explore this somewhat radical self-love? [e.g., yes, I'm willing to learn to make my self-talk loving and learn to embrace all my experiences]

2. In what situation do you find it hardest to love your-self without criticism and / or avoidance? [e.g., when I come out low in a business deal, I feel like I'm not on top of it enough]

_____

_____

_____

_____

3. What would the voice of encouragement say to you in this situation? [e.g., you were honest and opti-mistic--things that make the world a better place]

_____

_____

_____

_____

4. What is there to be grateful for in this situation? [e.g., by not belaboring the deal, I had time for other more enjoyable and important things in life]

_____

_____

_____

_____

5. Can you open to loving all aspects of yourself and your experience in this situation? [e.g., I'm glad that I haven't spent years learning the machinations of dominating in business deals--that's not really the kind of person I want to be; I love that I showed up and was honest and I'm glad to pay extra money and have my fulfilling life]

_____

_____

_____

_____

10:

Technique 8 Indecision at Conflicting Options

Indecision most often occurs because of conflicts between competing ideals of our thought-based identity. Before elaborating further, let's go straight to an example.

Example: Daughter's Orchestra Performance vs. Work Deadline

Suppose my job has a deadline the same night my daughter performs in the school orchestra. On the surface, it might seem that I simply want to be in two places at the same time. But if I'm anxious about having to choose, then most likely two or more parts of my thought-based identity are in conflict. My anxiety points to aspects of my thought-based identity that seem tenuous if I don't do both activities. It's not simply that they are both important to me. I'm anxious because I'm projecting a negative outcome as a result of not fulfilling one of the options. True Being emerges from the wellspring of abundant care and support for all and is certain that the flow of life works things out. Our thought-based identity, on the other hand, fails when it doesn't live up to its standards.

So how do I use this type of conflict to ferret out my thought-based identity? I notice how each option represents a part of my thought-based identity. In this case I believe "I'm a loving mom who goes to her daughter's performances," and I believe "I'm a reliable effective worker who delivers on time." If I can't do both of my options, then I'm failing at one of my beliefs, and furthermore I'm giving other people substantiating evidence of my failing. My thought-based identity survives on agreement from other people. So you see, conflicting aspects of my thought-based identity are confusing my decision and creating my anxiety.

Now suppose I drop any need to prove anything. Instead, I deepen into true Being and into the knowing that everyone has all the support they need. I surrender any control over how other people perceive me or even how I perceive myself. I become free to listen to my heart and tune into what is aligned with life's flow in this moment. Whatever choice I make, I do so without defense and with an open heart. The confusion and conflict drop away.

Example: Settle with Bouquet or Keep Searching

Here's another simple example. I wanted to buy flowers for a friend who'd helped me. I was to be at her place at 9:30 am and gave myself an extra hour to pick up flowers near her place. The first florist I went to was closed for the morning; the second florist had incorrectly listed their address. The third florist had a very limited selection, so the bouquet I bought there wasn't as nice as I'd hoped for.

Heading to her office, I was torn between saying, "I'm sorry the flowers aren't as great as I hoped; I tried three florists, and these flowers were the best I could find," which would likely diminish her enjoyment of the bouquet as I shared my struggle and criticized the bouquet, or going to a fourth florist and being late. I was indecisive because two different self-concepts conflicted with each other. My first self-concept was, "I show I care and am on time." This self-concept preferred arriving on time and apologizing for the bouqet. The second self-concept was, "I show I care by giving good gifts." This second self-concept preferred going to a fourth florist. I decided to simply enjoy the moment with her without supporting either identity--I'd arrive on time with the "inferior" bouquet but not apologize. When I handed her the not-so-nice bouquet, I felt my ego's temerity then focused on her. She was warm and appreciative, and our conversation flowed to topics of her day. I enjoyed her appreciation and let her experience of the flowers be her experience. My ego didn't get to have its stand-out moment—it was a simple moment of appreciation of her. Had things gone exactly according to my plan, I probably would've been happy in the box of my egoic ideal; instead I was in the mystery of the present moment, curious and free.

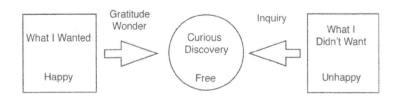

The steps of this practice are to

---

1. **Identify the separate options in an area where your feeling indecisive and anxious.**
2. **Identify how each option serves your thought-based identity.**
3. **Question the veracity of the assumptions of the thought-based identity.**
4. **Open to life with its unknowns rather than the prescriptions of the thought-based identity.**

When we're confused about competing choices, we can explore these options to identify the aspects of our thought-based identity that each serves. Once we see the thought-based identity in its attempts to serve itself, then we surrender our attempts to control and drop into true Being. What a gift our indecision turns out to be once it becomes a pathway into the present moment where what is is always enough!

Questions

1. Identify a specific situation where you're currently feeling indecisive or have recently been indecisive and describe the situation. [e.g., should I renew the expensive group membership?]

---

2. Identify your top options in this situation. [e.g., I can pay for the membership and maintain more networking opportunities or I can leave the group where I feel less aligned and often drained]

_____

_____

_____

_____

3. For each option, identify how the option serves your thought-based identity—makes you look good, keeps you safe, gives you something interesting, etc. [e.g., the membership keeps me in good standing with people I might otherwise lose contact with and leaving the group allows me to stay in my comfort zone and not be challenged so much]

_____

_____

_____

_____

4. Write the "I" statements that succinctly distill the primary concerns, the dominating aspect of yourself in each option, such as I keep my kids safe, I'm helpful, I'm free to do what I want, I take care of myself, etc. [e.g., "I keep up good connections" vs. "I am unique and have different perspectives than they do"]

_____

_____

_____

_____

5. Consider if none of the issues in number four above mattered, if they were all completely handled, permanently resolved. How would you be if you didn't have any of these concerns? [e.g., I would simply go where my energy flourished the most and trust the rest to work out]

_____

_____

_____

_____

6. Without these concerns, how would the situation of indecision change? How would you feel? Are there other options you didn't consider before? [e.g., I'd have no obligation to keep up the membership and I'd be happy to participate authentically when I did]

_____

_____

_____

_____

7. How would life be if you were less beholden to these expectations of your thought-based identity? [e.g., I'd follow life's movement of greatest interest and trust the flow; I'd feel grateful and light and life-affirming whichever way I chose; I wouldn't feel any need for "contacts"]

_____

_____

_____

_____

11:

Technique 9 Raising our Happiness Set Point

Happiness researchers have concluded that each person has their own happiness set point. In other words, we each have a happiness range that feels comfortable to us. Anything outside this range, more or less, feels uncomfortable. Having recognized this pattern, positive psychologists researched ways to help people raise their happiness set point and found that when people do kind things, they feel better about themselves and raise their happiness set point.

As we live from the free, vibrant flow of true Being, our happiness levels increase. Initially we'll find ourselves outside our comfort zone, and unconsciously we'll find something wrong, missing, or inadequate to return back to our comfort zone. For example, we'll criticize, act out, hype things up, or even numb out–almost anything to shift out of continual joy and contentment.

I've noticed that over a given period of time, say one week for example, our thought-based identity will dominate the stage of our consciousness with its discontent for some consistent average percentage of time. For discussion purposes, let's assume that it's 25% of the time. Whatever the percent, that percent becomes the comfort zone for our thought-based identity's need to assert its ideas of what "should" be different. (It may have other thoughts during other times.)

We go along at peace until it's time for our 25% to show up. Then we'll find something or someone in our world to point to as "threatening," "hurtful," "dangerous," "unjust," "boring," or any other number of complaints. It seems to us that the problem is entirely real and outside of ourselves, but with very close observation, we discover that our perception is biased and internally driven by our state of mind at the moment–we're simply filling our 25% quota.

When I first heard this concept, I didn't believe it. I scoffed to think that I purposely manufactured complaints from neutral circumstances. I was certain that I preferred being peaceful and happy. I knew (or so I thought) that the situations were the cause and that most people would agree that these upsetting situations were valid problems and were the origin of my complaints.

However, I respected the source of this concept (in my case, Victor Baranco founder of an intentional community that has now run for over fifty years). I also knew that the latter part of the principle–that when I argue with what is, I lose touch with true Being–was correct. So, I decided to test the hypothesis empirically. Was there anything in my experience to substantiate the idea that my reservations with how life was unfolding were internally driven by my state of mind rather than by external circumstances?

I uncovered the following four pieces of supportive evidence. Then as a final test, I developed new ways of being based on accepting the hypothesis as true, and they worked–they resulted in more awareness of true Being! The theory substantiated itself.

My four pieces of evidence were:

1. I noticed that each person has their own apparent disposition, their own most frequent emotional state (e.g., being mostly at peace, being troubled, being let-down, being put-out, etc.). When I compared different people with similar circumstances, it became more obvious that a person's disposition predicted their state (upset, peaceful, anxious, joyful, etc.) more reliably than their circumstances did. These observations supported the original

principle that our quota for unhappiness (stemming from our happiness set point) determines our emotional state more than our circumstances.

2. I noticed that the same situation could at times appear neutral, mildly annoying, or highly aggravating to me though nothing on the outside had substantially changed. I might be very aggravated by my puppy chewing up my books or I might let it slide. I might be very upset by my spouse being late or I might not be bothered at all, and so on. Clearly the situation wasn't the main determining factor for whether or not I was upset. Something else, perhaps my personal quota, was driving my level of equanimity.

3. I noticed a pattern: when I'd just reached a new high (spiritual opening, insight, or joy), it was often followed within twenty-four to forty-eight hours by upset. The quota theory supported that such upsets would happen. According to the theory, large injections of joy, insight, or well-being would throw off the 25%, so I'd unconsciously bring the average back to normal by some type of distress. I watched more closely and noticed that when I was especially happy, I frequently ended up upset in close succession. For **example**, arriving home from an enlightening, expansive workshop, I was suddenly

irritated by my partner's professorial-type mini lectures. I found this behavior of his at times adorable, at times inane, and at other times highly disagreeable. I linked my irritability after the workshop with my recent high. The quota theory was gaining support.

4. A very convincing piece of evidence showed up. A situation happened that was mildly upsetting. Just as possible responses were coming to mind, I caught a quiet little thought that said, "I'll remember that situation for later when I need something to be upset about." The thought was so subtle that I felt like a curtain had been opened to a subconscious part of my mind's inner workings. Astonished, I stopped in my tracks. Not only were my egoic thought patterns selectively choosing when to be upset, but they were planning in advance for those occasions.

I was convinced.

Then I applied the theory to my benefit. If my thought-based identity maintained itself by showing up as resistance to reality 25% of the time, then perhaps I could reset my 25% to 22% or even 19%! So the next time I caught myself getting irritated, I decided to be intensely present with the irritability without acting on it. I saw the irritability for what it was, an attempt to maintain my quota, so I waited it out and let it pass, watching its energy rise in my body and then eventually subside. The energy often feels antsy, rambunctious, hot, and pressurized. Deep breaths, movement, a warm bath or shower, and grounding through my feet can help it pass a little faster, but it still can take quite a while. Nevertheless, it eventually subsides, and in that moment a new groove forms in the pathways of my subconscious! My old rut is still there, but a new option to counter upset with spaciousness is now available.

By repeatedly not complying with the demands of the quota and instead sensing the egoic energy without investing in it, I gradually reset the quote. Following this theory works. Now I notice upset and see it for what it is, a momentary need to reestablish my separate sense of self. Feeling uncomfortable at times is a good sign, a sign that I'm outside my normal quota.

I no longer believe things are wrong externally. When upsets arise, I regularly deepen into presence and acknowledge my habit of periodically imagining a "better alternate reality" (e.g., where someone was kinder, something happened more easily, etc.). I may even say aloud to myself, as a gentle noticing, "So you want to feel in control right now." Or, "you want to feel small right now." Or, "you want to be owed something right now." Everyone has their own feeling tone. In these moments, I bring awareness to the fixation on unavailable alternatives and envelop it in presence. As I sit with the discomfort of a new behavior (attention without reactivity), I welcome the discomfort because it indicates that I'm pushing the envelope of my previous comfort zone, my previous 25% quota, and I celebrate.

Essentially I attend to the arising complaint with curiosity and presence but without belief or reaction. (Attending without belief is distinct from suppression which would shove the feelings down and force a false facade.) The more I've enveloped complaints in presence, the more peace has increased in my life. I've gently loosened my habitual grip on complaining thought patterns by seeing through their hidden agenda (creating a separate sense of self) and increased my happiness set point.

Our thought-based identity causes suffering by jumping to assumptions that things that have already happened shouldn't have happened. It defends these assumptions with rules about how people should and shouldn't treat us, etc. Once something has happened, to argue with it is like banging our head on a wall. It takes a very open mind and heart to find the gift or learning in every situation. Once we do so, we can take the next step peacefully rather than being burdened by reactivity or vengeance.

Example: Working Months Without a Paycheck

As a simple example, I worked for an organization for ten months before they paid me. I knew from the beginning that the organization was still completing its legal paperwork to establish itself, so I expected it to take time (and had the financial buffer to be okay). But after five months, I was disgruntled. I confirmed that they were still working on the paperwork, but I was still upset.

I started noting to myself whenever the upset arose, "you want to feel separate and autonomous right now" and then would bring spacious awareness to my inner experience as I watched the separating process of wishing to be paid more promptly. I was essentially imagining a me separate from the benevolent flow, a me who thought she knew better. Without judgment or reactivity toward the upset, I held the disgruntled experience graciously as it came and went and later came and went again with its own rhythm, eventually subsiding over a couple months.

To sit with my upset at not being paid was enlightening! Over and over I watched my "should-be" beliefs about what I deserved and noticed my habitual attempts at separation! The more I understood how my separation quota was at work, the more it shifted. Awareness and peace took its place, costing me nothing but patience.

To attend to complaints without reaction doesn't mean I become a doormat. Once I'm at peace, I can choose to move away from someone in equanimity without making them wrong. For example, I had a close friend who repeatedly complained that I hadn't honored his requests well enough. At first, I defended myself and made him wrong. Then I applied this process and came to see that he had to say what he felt. When I no longer found him wrong, I found myself more compassionate and objective in the matter. I made the changes that seemed appropriate, but his complaints persisted. I saw his suffering and felt increasing compassion for him even as his complaints escalated. Eventually he stormed off, and when he tried to resume frequent visits, I said that it was time for us to move on. I no longer believed that he or I should be different, and accepting us each as we were, it was clear to me that our time together had run its course.

Every time we want something or someone (including ourselves) to be different than they are, we comply with our quota of discontent, or as one friend called it, "our misery quota," which closely aligns with the pain-body described by Eckhart Tolle. Furthermore, when we blame people, we create "wrong-doers" in our world. This separation is painful for us and supports our mental identity. If we pause and sit without reactivity, we may come to see that at worst "wrong-doers" are merely people who are confused and are trying to make things work out for themselves and those they love. When we perceive another person as malevolent, we mentally attack them and reality. Recall the last time someone blamed you and considered you a "wrong-doer" of some sort or another. Their judgment felt painful unless you had no sense of identity operating at the moment. To treat people as doing the best they know in possible confusion spares us from the painful separation of blame and judgment. To treat people with understanding isn't to say that there aren't societal consequences for behavior. When certain behaviors happen (e.g. intentional crimes), other behaviors usually follow in response (societal consequences). Nevertheless we can peacefully give people the freedom to have their own journey (with the consequences) and love them, whether from up close or from afar.

In summary, this technique is to

---

1. **Notice your habits of being upset and not upset, often about something that hasn't changed much.**

2. **Notice when upset arises and acknowledge it.**

3. **See if you can postpone the upset for several minutes or even wait it out altogether, bringing**

presence to the body sensations accompanying the upset.

4. **Congratulate yourself for your discomfort! You are resetting your happiness set point!**

Once we see our quota at work and start to shift our happiness set point, we increase our attunement with true Being. The price of arguing with reality is separation and suffering. The price of joy is giving up the right to make anything wrong.

Questions

1. Can you identify something that bothers you at some times and not at other times? [e.g., when my partner procrastinates]

---

2. The next time you start to feel upset about some-thing, try waiting before expressing the upset or acting on the upset for three minutes. How did that feel? [e.g., very uncomfortable, a lot of motion and tension in the body]

_____

_____

_____

_____

3. What is an example of how discomfort might be a positive sign for you that a habit is loosening? [e.g., I can see how emotionally venting just contin-ues the cycle and how being with the inner tension could rechannel it]

_____

_____

_____

_____

4. Try delaying your upset for at least three minutes every time you start to feel upset. Acknowledge the subconscious intent to feel separate as you pause. [e.g., I see how criticizing my partner gives me an unneeded sense of superiority--definitely separating on multiple levels]

_____

_____

_____

_____

5. How might getting upset serve your thought-based identity? [e.g., I feel how my upset is a way of asserting myself that isn't based in reality--I don't need the sense of control]

_____

_____

_____

_____

12:

Technique 10 Identify Our Habitual Ways of Being

The next approach for dismantling our thought-based identity is to recognize a habitual way of being that has become a blind spot.

We have habitual ways of operating that are so comfortable and automatic that we may not realize that we don't have flexibility in these areas. When following these habits, we reflexively follow our ingrained patterns rather than being available and attuned to the moment.

As examples, we may be an effective achiever, always aware of our to-do list, or we may be a procrastinator frequently letting things somehow work themselves out while we focus on our preferred activities, or we may be a teaser with a joke ready for any tense situation. These old stand-bys can be so seemingly helpful that we don't notice our constant go-to position that automatically steps in without us attuning to the moment. This collection of our habitual ways of being can be called our "me suit." (Justin Taylor, a meditation teacher) Often it takes a challenge from someone else to bring our habits to our attention.

Once someone has pointed out one of our habitual patterns, we have a golden opportunity to dismantle another structure that prevents our intimacy with true Being and the flow of life. The steps to dismantling them are as follows:

1. We inventory the toll that our habit takes in our lives and especially in our relationships. As someone who identified with being an effective achiever, I noticed the following costs in my life:

    a. My expectations of myself regularly caused stress in my day-to-day activities as I tried to do it all well.

    b. When reality didn't fall together despite my best intentions, I'd take out my frustration on others, being impatient, short, and critical.

    c. I found myself feeling superior to others who didn't have their stuff together.

    d. I'd go to great lengths to take care of details just to be sure that I looked good, even prioritizing my achievement over being available for my loved ones and for myself.

In fact, we may discover the habitual way of being by noticing these costs in our lives. If we're frequently stressed over the same types of situations or unavailable for open-hearted interactions with our loved ones, we look to see if there is a repeating concern (such as looking good) and habitual way of being (such as achieving, joking, etc.) that pulls us out of the flow of present moment awareness.

2. We test to see how willing we are to do the opposite (especially if we aren't sure whether or not it's a habit for us). For example, if we're attached to our to-do list, we can purposely let a few things slide, or if we procrastinate, we can do three things promptly as soon as we become aware that they need to be done. If we tease or joke, we can stay serious through a couple conversations. As we do the test of doing the opposite, we observe our inner state very closely. What emotions come up? Do we experience any resistance or anxiety or inner conflict? This discomfort is evidence that we're dealing with a habit that limits our range of responsiveness. Such habits are building blocks of our thought-based identity.

Example: Never Cancelling Plans

Personally, I caught myself never cancelling my plans with people even when new circumstances arose that made keeping the commitment stressful. Over and over I kept my difficult appointments. When the other person cancelled, I felt egoic pride that I hadn't been the one to cancel—I'd preserved my identity as "reliable." I noticed the comparing, the superiority, and the resulting separation in my relating. Clearly I was prioritizing the thought-based identity over true Being. So I dropped this identity and started cancelling when needed. The first conversations were difficult—I was very apologetic and hypersensitive to any disappointment on the other person's part. Miraculously, the other person was usually very gracious, and as a result I felt closer to them. I no longer projected my rigid demands onto them, and I noticed the natural caring and flexibility already present in my friends that I hadn't fully appreciated before. Through surrendering the idea of myself as "reliable," I became more present and connected. My heart opened more, I engaged more authentically, and flow increased in my life and relationships.

3. Having noticed how our habits impact our lives and experimented with other ways of being, we then consistently practice new ways of being and notice what opens up. Those who leap into action may practice waiting and following the inner, still voice; those who hesitate to act may practice coming forward and engaging; those who joke may practice being more

open with themselves and others. When we step outside of comfortable habits, we engage our curiosity
and touch into the unknown. We loosen our attempts
at control and become more emotionally available to
others and to the flow of the moment. Rather than
following robotic instincts, we become more vibrant
and free.

Dropping our guard, we respond authentically as life
moves us. We may find ourselves moved to joy or moved
to tears, each moment differently. Our full range of responses is more attuned to the uniqueness of the moment, flowing from curiosity, to yes, to no, and so on. We
give ourselves freedom to be all of it.

Whenever we notice ourselves back in our old groove,
we invite ourselves to be more present and attuned,
bringing our full awareness to the moment, softening and
opening so that we move freely with the flow of true Being.

In summary, this practice is to

---

1. **Identify a personal habit and inventory the toll
   it takes in your life and relationships.**

2. **Try a couple test runs of doing something else
   and notice if and how it makes you feel uncomfortable. (If you're always equally willing to do
   the opposite, then you probably haven't found
   a habitual way of being and should look again.)**

3. **Practice using opposite responses that loosen the way of being and develop more attunement and responsiveness to life and relationships.**

Present and Attuned

To better understand what it means to be present and attuned, imagine you're touching a slab of an unknown material to determine what it is. Your senses would heighten as you felt just how hard it is, how cold it is, what sound it makes when tapped, etc. Typically, we stay open like this only for a short while until we've categorized the material, and then we turn our senses to other things as our past knowledge and beliefs take the place of fully experiencing the material. Now suppose we didn't move on to categorization; suppose we instead stayed with our open awareness without imposing any structure onto the experience–this openness is an example of being present and attuned. So to be present and attuned with people, we have this same open attentiveness in conversations with others. Rather than having expectations for the conversation, we're curious about the other person's moment-to-moment experience as well as our own dynamically changing experience. We focus on understanding, letting the outcome evolve organically. When we're present and attuned, we're undefended, open-hearted, and aware. We become intimate with the flow of whatever is happening in this moment, one with the aliveness of reality, open and free.

Questions:

1. If possible, ask a loved one what might be a habitual way of being that you use. If asking someone isn't an option, review what stresses you avoid in life and identify a habitual way you try to reduce these stresses. [e.g., I avoid confrontation]

_____

_____

_____

_____

2. List the costs of using this habit in your life and in your relationships. [e.g., I withdraw in confrontational situations, feel run over, and am not authentic]

_____

_____

_____

_____

3. List ways that you could try another way of being. [e.g., I could say "something here isn't sitting well with me, can I get back to you about it?" or I could stomp my foot or I could raise my voice and say "I don't want to argue with you"]

_____

_____

_____

_____

4. Plan three situations where you'll try out these new options. [e.g., I'll talk to my co-worker who doesn't seem to pull her share, I'll talk to my neighbor who often parks where it's hard for me to reverse out of my driveway, I'll talk to my friend who says she wants to grow but has been complaining about the same thing now for four months]

_____

_____

_____

_____

5. What happened in yourself and in your life as a result of these experiments? [e.g., people were happy to be noticed, and some good conversations resulted and a load was lifted from me]

_____

_____

_____

_____

6. In those same types of situations, are you willing to embrace new ways of being different from those habits? [e.g., yes, I look forward to continuing to take more baby steps in not avoiding conflict]

_____

_____

_____

_____

Technique 11 The Avoided Conversation

So often we have a small unresolved issue with someone close to us, and we don't want to deal with it. We may not even identify exactly why we're avoiding the conversation. This little topic often hides a constricted area that hasn't yet opened to the fullness of true Being. We can turn our unresolved issue into an opportunity for fuller expression of true Being with a two-part process, an internal part and an external part.

Example: My Husband Spent Too Much Time Helping His Friends

To begin with the internal part, I identify who or what I'm making wrong, inquire into my assumptions in the situation, and then love any constricted areas that show up within myself. For example, I didn't like how much time my husband was spending helping some friends when it seemed he was behind on some of his own responsibilities. So I first questioned my belief that he should be attending to his own responsibilities more and his friends less. I saw that I really couldn't say which was best. I also saw that I wanted him to attend to his responsibilities because I wanted to know that I could rely on him if I needed help. I was concerned that if his affairs were disorganized, I might not have him to rely on. I noticed the fear underlying this apparent need. I turned my love toward this fearful part for a few days (bringing the fear to mind from time to time and bathing it in love) until the fearful part relaxed. Without the assumption that I needed his affairs to be organized, I no longer saw his allocation of time as wrong.

Having resolved my concerns (the internal part), I checked again about whether there was anything left to discuss (the external part). I was still curious about my husband's choices. So I took time to sense into true Being and then asked him what was his purpose in spending additional days helping his friends after the major assistance was complete. As I asked this question, I noticed my own body sensations, thoughts, and emotions. Were there any tensions? I noticed them and opened, relaxing through it all.

Then I heard his answer. Again, I noticed my own body sensations, thoughts, and emotions. My first judgment was that he really hadn't thought it through very much, which came with a tightness in my gut. I questioned my certainty about what I thought would have been better, turned loving attention toward my tight gut and paused, allowing myself to open and relax. I admitted to myself that I didn't know what was best for him. Once I'd relaxed again, I noticed that it felt helpful for both of us that we give the situation some more consideration.

Feeling open again, I asked another question about how he might be underestimating the maturity and self-sufficiency of his friends. As I asked the question, I noticed my thoughts, body sensations, and emotions, checking to see where I was closed in any way and gently breathed into it all, allowing myself to relax.

During his reply, I again noticed my thoughts, body sensations, and emotions. I heard him make some points I hadn't previously considered, and he seemed to clarify his own thinking as he verbalized his understanding of their situation. After another round of question and answer, the conversation ended. There was no plan of action or specific outcome. Instead, there was greater peace and understanding. I better understood and appreciated his care for his friends. He noticed his tendency to project helplessness that wasn't there.

The end result was connection, openness, and freedom where there had been avoidance and even resentment. Human relating continually invites us into the unknown, into the mystery of love and life. Every place that we avoid actually invites us to open to the mystery and discover the sweetness naturally here if we just look and inquire.

In summary, the practice here is to

---

1. **Identify a conversation you're avoiding.**
2. **Identify the trigger in the conversation.**
3. **Inquire to understand the trigger.**
4. **Question the confusion underlying the trigger (what you think is wrong) until a new perspective opens up.**
5. **Once the trigger has lost its potency, reevaluate if there is something still to discuss.**
6. **If there is still something to discuss, use questions to increase understanding.**
7. **With every question and answer, pay close attention to arising thoughts, body sensations, and emotions.**
8. **Keep the conversation slow, with plenty of time for noticing at each step.**
9. **Breathe into constrictions and concerns as they arise, taking time to hold them in love and to allow them to arise, be noticed, and dissipate.**
10. **Focus on increasing understanding without attachment to particular outcomes.**

Through this process, we inquire to cultivate peace around a trigger, we love ourselves, and we have a conversation that is open-hearted and curious. At every point in the conversation we attend to our own thoughts, sensations, and emotions so as to bring them into awareness as the conversation progresses. As we own our internal reactions and bring loving presence to them, we have the space to remain curious and open-hearted and to cultivate understanding rather than pushing for a particular outcome. In so doing we tap into connection and to the organic movement of true Being, a flow of dynamic aliveness.

Questions:

1. What conversation are you avoiding? [e.g, my partner has been moody for a couple months now]

_____

_____

_____

_____

2. What are your concerns about the situation? [e.g., I never know if I'm going to get the nice version or the testy version]

_____

_____

_____

_____

3. Who or what do you see as "wrong" or needing to be fixed? [e.g., my partner should be the nice version most of the time]

_____

_____

_____

_____

4. Are you certain you know best? [e.g., I really don't know what she's going through]

_____

_____

_____

_____

5. How might your own fears be confounding the situation? [e.g., I'm afraid she loves me less or is unhappy with me; I find myself avoiding her]

_____

_____

_____

_____

6. Can you love the fearful part of yourself? [e.g., yes, my inner child can be afraid of being overlooked, I'll love my little one]

_____

_____

_____

_____

7. Are you willing to see that your apparent need might be satisfied in other ways? [e.g., I can be more deliberate about listening to music, talking to friends, and doing activities that are uplifting rather than zoning out]

_____

_____

_____

_____

8. Once you feel more open regarding the situation, is there anything remaining to discuss? [e.g., I feel much more supported as I've changed my own behaviors, and I'm still wondering what might be bothering her, but I feel lighter now]

_____

_____

_____

9. If so, tune into true Being and let yourself be curious about the other person as well as about your own thoughts, body sensations, and emotions. Have the conversation slowly, checking in with yourself at each step. Give yourself and the other the time and loving attention to hold any constrictions, judgments, or fears that come up. [e.g., I ask her if something has been up for her over the past weeks and feel nervous and then breathe and relax as I listen]

_____

_____

_____

10. Continue the conversation in this way toward understanding without a particular outcome in mind. [e.g., she admits to frustrations at work mostly and extra tasks at home that I hadn't noticed; I feel nervous that maybe she blames me and then breathe into the anxiety; I ask if she wants help from me and listen; she does so much I just want to hug her]

---

11. Afterwards, notice what you learned about yourself and about the situation. What flowed organically as a result of the discussion? How did curiosity and openness contribute to the new understanding? [e.g., we felt much closer after the conversation, I wasn't defensive, we had a great hug; I think she feels less stressed too]

14:

Technique 12 It's All Me

Example: Subway Ticket Scam

While on my way to appointment, I went to make a purchase at a subway ticket machine in New York City. In the middle of my transaction, a man next to me reached over, cancelled my transaction, and asked me to buy a ticket from him instead. I refused and started a new transaction. Again, halfway through the transaction, the man reached over and cancelled it. This time I emphatically explained why I needed to use the machine, and I started my transaction again. A third time he cancelled it, this time elaborating more assertively why his ticket was a special deal. Because I believed that I should be as agreeable as possible, saying, "No," so many times had worn me down. I rolled my eyes and agreed to do business with him.

He looked me in the eye and said, "Trust me." After taking my payment, he courteously ran the ticket through the subway ticket reader allowing me to enter, and then handed the ticket to me through the gate. It was supposed to be good for a whole month of unlimited rides, but as you've probably guessed, it was a bad ticket. It wasn't good for even one more ride. I'd been duped, or so I thought. I felt stupid, taken advantage of, and wronged. I was furious with myself and with the man. I was so angry it seemed my whole day was ruined by my disgust.

However, I wasn't willing to give up the day to anger. I had to clear my upset somehow! It really seemed a cut-and-dry bad situation, yet I went to work to use it for my own clarity. I started by considering the man. He was a real crook in my eyes, a liar and a cheat. Here was my challenge. Could I somehow see that he *should* be exactly as he was, doing exactly what he did? Recognizing the fundamental connection common to all humans, I surmised that he was more like me than different. My experience is that at the core we are similar beings with different challenges, different histories, and different skills. Could I find any place inside me that would steal from someone else? To identify with him was a real puzzle, a deep dive into creativity. How could I find any place in me that could behave as he had?

I opened meditatively. For me to steal from someone else, I'd have to be desperate, and I'd have to think the other person wasn't hurt by my stealing. Could I think of such a scenario? I imagined being at a huge dinner buffet where the participants were allowed unlimited helpings of gourmet food. Then I imagined that I was not a participant but a starving onlooker who somehow got access to the room. I could see myself in those circumstances stealing someone's abandoned plate of food, knowing that they could very easily get as many other plates of food as they wanted. It would be a no-brainer. In the room of eighty people or more, my plateful would be of no consequence. Then compassion flooded my heart. Did that man feel so desperate as to see no better option than to steal? Did he see me as having much easier access to earning money than he had? I don't know, but I felt certain that his sense of himself regarding money was closer to that mentality than to my own confidence. My anger toward him subsided; I was sure he saw no better option.

I still felt duped, stupid, and diminished. Here was my second hurdle. I had to kindly explore what could be right about my apparent stupidity? Again, it was a puzzle, requiring a longer meditative pause. Finally, I saw that my effort in saying, "No" was what had worn me down. I didn't like saying, "No." As long as I had a preference for saying, "Yes," and being agreeable, I couldn't be free. The many situations of life require every type of response from me. If I have no thought-based identity (such as "I'm an agreeable person") to protect, then I'm free to flow into any response as appropriate to the situation. I could happily say, "No," over and over. Here was my lesson. This man had confronted my attachment to being agreeable. Wow! I dropped the need to be agreeable like a hot potato! Who knew what next situation might come my way requiring a definite "No!" I opened myself to flowing into "No!" whenever necessary–perhaps the next situation would cost me a lot more if I couldn't say, "No." I felt so empowered.

Continuing with my day, I was free! I had no lingering bitterness toward the man who clearly was doing the best he knew to do. I was free in any future situation to say, "No," whenever appropriate! A "No" can come as easily as a "Yes." That subway ticket price was actually the price for my personal customized workshop in saying, "No."

This practice is to

---

1. **Identify someone who you think has wronged you.**
2. **Imagine a situation (it might be pretty extreme) where you'd do the equivalent of what that person has done.**

3. **Consider how you'd feel if all your other options seemed even worse than that option.**

4. **Consider the pain and confusion that the other person is likely experiencing and see if you're willing to be compassionate toward the person.**

5. **Consider if there is anything for you to learn for possible future similar situations.**

The power of this exercise emerged when I assumed that he and I were not fundamentally different. We simply had different backgrounds, needs, and perspectives. It's easy to see others (a politician on the other side for example) as the enemy. We imagine giant gulfs between ourselves and others. And because no such gulf exists, it is exhausting and painful to sustain the idea of the gulf. Whatever I see someone else do, I can find the place in me that might at some time and circumstance be drawn to do the same.

When I started seeing others as fundamentally the same as me, I opened to a world of compassion, humility and fundamental unity. In any situation, I've learned that the other person is not as "other" as I initially assume. Through this practice, we recognize the commonalities of humanness and find ourselves disarmed. We open to the love already there. We also discover freedom to respond appropriately without having to make the other person wrong.

Questions:

1. Can you remember an interaction with someone you considered a bad person? [e.g., a internet service sales person dishonestly presented the plan]

_____

_____

_____

_____

2. What did the person do? (List the actions without elaborating the intentions and malevolent wishes toward you.) [e.g., he gave me pricing for a plan without TV service then enrolled me in a more expensive plan with TV service and emphasized that I should set up automatic payments]

_____

_____

_____

_____

3. Can you imagine any situation or circumstance when you might be tempted to do similar actions? What desperate condition might throw you into considering a similar behavior? (Again, remove intentions from the scenario.) Take your time to be as creative as needed. [e.g., if I had loved ones to provide for and selling on commission was the only job that could help me provide a nice life for them]

_____

_____

_____

_____

4. How does your discovery of such a situation throw light on the confusion under which the other person might be operating? [e.g., he's probably too preoccupied to give any consideration to the money lost by customers who are over-charged for services not used]

_____

_____

_____

_____

5. What way of being in you is the opposite fit to the other person's way of being? (e.g., over helping versus over demanding, self-questioning versus dominating, feeling ashamed versus over criticism) Can you see how this attribute is how you play along in such scenarios? [e.g., I like to be trusting and generous and don't want to waste my time]

_____

_____

_____

_____

6. What wisdom do you now have about handling these situations in the future? Can you forgive yourself for not having that wisdom at the time? [e.g., the money I lost is part of the whole financial system we have where some of my retirement accounts are probably invested in companies that

have some sales tactics I wouldn't like; the way of it now is a lot of financial entanglement; I'll do the best I can to keep things in the open]

---

7. What can you be grateful for as you re-evaluate that situation? [e.g., I'm so grateful that in this scenario, I'm not the one on the other side; sometimes I have been the cheater, but it's so much better not to be the cheater this time]

15:

Technique 13 The Movie Test

A simple test to see beyond my thought-based identity's dislike of a situation to the unconditional appreciation of true Being is what I'll call the movie test. "Would I enjoy watching a movie of someone who works through my current situation and comes to a happy ending?" Over and over I find that I answer, "Yes!" When that happens, I tap into the part of me that finds this situation fascinating as long as it isn't truly dangerous. In fact, no situation is dangerous for true Being, so that fascination is more reality-based than my resistance toward the situation.

(To clarify, most things we avoid threaten our thought-based identity, not our physical body. Of course, I avoid putting my physical body in danger. As much as I can, I take care of my body as a wonderful gift, and when things beyond my control harm my body, I get the best help I can while serenely remaining in the knowing that true Being hasn't been damaged.)

Example: Friend with "Personality Disorder"

For example, I have a friend who has what psychologists would call a personality disorder. From time to time, I became exasperated interacting with him, even to the point of wanting to shut him out of my life. So I asked myself one day, "Would I enjoy a movie about someone with his personality disorder?" Yes! I like movies about people with apparent mental disorders—their initially eccentric or inscrutable points of view fascinate me. I also discover profound compassion once I understand what it's like to be inside their experience.

Taking time meditatively to recognize myself as eternal indestructible Being, I see that I have nothing to be harmed by interacting with my friend, and I'm excited to watch the movie up front and center; I get to live it. With this knowing, my resistance collapses, and I feel curious and gracious. I follow inner wisdom in spending time with him rather than self-protecting. I sit with him and hear his anxiety, confusion, fear, blame, and certainty that if others were different, he would be okay. When I offer an alternative viewpoint, I feel no openness in him, so I return to listening. Eventually the topic changes to something else, and then the conversation ends.

In a future conversation, he blames me for trying to be an authority in his life. I apologize and offer that he's doing perfectly well on his own with no input from me. I can't know what is best for him. At times he seems to grasp an inner wisdom and find periods of greater equanimity. At other times he focuses more on the thoughts of despair. Whatever happens, I know that at his core he's eternal Being and in no danger. Moreover, he's teaching me the willingness of Being to experience suffering. True Being is the core of essence running through darkness as well as light.

In another conversation his hurt and despair fill him with blame of others, of himself, and of me. It seems to me that the yearning underlying his suffering harkens back to the true Being, from which he's unconsciously detached. I hear his pain and feel the isolation that results from his demands that life be different. Each complaint is another brick in the wall that isolates him from true Being, and he can't stop himself. I sit silently loving him in his confusion. I learn how to remain spacious through each conversation, completely disarmed, caring and available, silent, and with an increasing knowing that Being is no less when it's in disguise than when it's out in the open.

Over the years he approaches and pulls back. I don't take anything personally. I see the miracle as peace grows in his life. I'm grateful for him, my teacher. No confusion has to be fixed. Being has its own timing, its own path, its own adventure. My words are of no consequence. I feel the vastness of Being flowing between us both, holding us in its mystery. He's easy to love when I see nothing wrong. I love my meditations when he calls me full of hurt, and I love when he calls me more at peace. With no ego to be harmed, life is a fascinating adventure.

To summarize, this practice is to

---

1. **Identify a situation that you wish were different.**

2. **Imagine a movie with that situation as the plot line and that has a happy ending. Would you enjoy such a movie?**

3. **Consider that as true Being, you're a living happy ending. So, relax and enjoy the show.**

Questions

1. What relationship or situation do you wish you could remove from your life? [e.g., my teammate at work who is always late so my time is wasted and we get off schedule]

---

2. What is the worst eventuality you're afraid of in this relationship or situation? [e.g., I will have frenzied periods at work that could have been easily avoided]

---

3. What would the occurrence of that eventuality mean about yourself? How might you blame, what might you assume, over what would you be disappointed? [e.g., I think of myself as a peaceful person who is on time and responsible; my co-worker's actions result in me not living out my preference]

---

4. Have you ever been interested in a movie that covered a similar situation or relationship? What intrigued you in the movie? [e.g., I have watched many movies where there was frenzied action--it can be very exciting]

_____

_____

_____

_____

5. If you were free of the future projections and fear triggered by the situation or relationship and were certain that infinite wisdom guided the situation, what aspects of the situation or relationship would become interesting? [e.g., I can see work as naturally alternating between smooth and rushed in an unavoidable cycle that is exciting if I don't worry

about it. I can have steady periods and I can have rushed periods, and I can still be peaceful as I'm rushing, it doesn't have to mean anything]

_____

_____

_____

_____

6. If you allowed this curiosity to flow through you, how would you be more clearly in touch with true Being? [e.g., I might laugh as I rushed finding it a silly part of life or feel energized by it; either way, the rushing would be an experience I'm having not a challenge to my idea of how a peaceful person should be]

_____

_____

_____

_____

7. Can you find a part of yourself that is willing to experiment with curiosity rather than trying to fix the situation or relationship? [e.g., yes, and now that I'm not so fixated on her, I might even be able to find someone else to fill in the gap before she arrives]

_____

_____

_____

_____

16:

Technique 14 Seeing Beyond Linear Time

Our experience of time as humans is different than the experience of time as true Being. Physics, science fiction, and our dreams all give us mini glimpses of other ways that time might be experienced or stepped outside of altogether.

Experiencing life from the perspective of true Being, we discover that each moment is a complete masterpiece, a perfect culmination needing nothing more. However, our time-limited perception often can't wrap itself around the full beauty and natural balance of all that is.

I've found that playing with my concepts of time helps me open into gratitude, wonder, and freedom. Here are three examples of how playing with my understanding of time changed my perspectives.

Seeing the Bigger Picture

Just like one page is not the book, one day in a situation is not the whole occurrence. To get a fuller perspective, we let some time pass to better understand the balance and harmony of the situation. If we could simultaneously experience all time, all space, and all dimensions, we'd know how awesome that balance is. (Of course, paradoxically, true Being can likewise be experienced in a microscopic point in a nanosecond.) With only our human space-time perception, however, we may see only small segments that seem confusing.

Without seeing the rest of the picture, we may argue with reality, but we can remind ourselves that perfection may be clearer as we curiously observe its apparent process of unfolding. With patience we develop an expanded perspective, and in hindsight we see apparent problems transform into gifts as we recognize the benevolent choreography lying just below the surface.

Example: Inter-Departmental Conflicts

For example, I worked at a company when a change of management brought in several leaders who apparently wanted to rush in and fix declining performance. Morale was low, and inter-department cooperation declined. The old-timers in particular were not forthcoming with their expertise and wisdom. At first I saw this situation as a stalemated power struggle within a static monolith separate from me. I wasn't tuned in to the bud of renewal that was already there, yet to emerge more tangibly.

Looking beyond my frozen, me-and-them perception, I changed paradigms and saw myself as an integral creative part of this evolving corporation. As a result, I saw that, just as I'd been judging everyone else, I was also withholding my wisdom. So, first I set down on paper what I saw as important for our future. I understood that this vision was the universe flowing through me in the evolution of the organization. Then, I identified areas of strength that I appreciated in each of the top leaders of the organization. I realized that if I were to work with them, I'd meet with them more effectively from a place of appreciation of their contribution to the organization. Feeling more integrated with the organization, I next met individually with over ten of the executives (some several levels my senior) and suggested that we celebrate past achievements and use them as a launching point for our next improvements. I didn't see an immediate response to my meetings, but three months later, we had a company-wide meeting that followed my idea exactly! No one else had seen the problem as I did because they brought different strengths to the table. I was the one to have my particular perspective, and I shared it in a way that valued them and offered possible next steps. That celebratory meeting was a turning point.

All the world is evolving as one whole in an apparently time-limited unfolding, but we more easily appreciate the implicit balance of true Being, which is always present, with the passing of time. Returning to my corporate example, all the ingredients of cooperation were already present when I criticized the company—just like a trimmed-back rose bush has all the elements of a full rose bush, only at a different stage of expression. Once I joined in and appreciated the strengths of the whole team, the fuller expression of cooperation became clearer in time.

The Experience of Growth

Our experience in linear time leads to another common confusion regarding growth. As humans, we grow and learn and generally enjoy doing so. By definition growth means that we gain new insight. We can then apply this learning in our future. But often we try to apply it to our past and feel regretful, guilty, angry, blaming, etc., even though we (and the people around us) didn't know better at the time (otherwise, it would've happened differently). For the past to conform with our current ideals, we'd have to have had all current wisdom in the past, but then we'd no longer have the experience of growth. Yet isn't growth an enjoyable part of the experience of linear time? So we seem to want growth and also want to already have all wisdom, clearly a set up for disappointment. Growth, it turns out, is our current experience.

Example: Comparing Parenting Styles

For example, at times my parents tended toward a disciplined, high-expectations style of parenting as they raised me. I'm the oldest of four, so by the time the youngest came around, they'd developed more flexibility. I might have been unhappy with the contrast between her experience of my parents and my own. However, no matter how good their parenting was of me, it was naturally even better six years and three children later! As it turns out, they were the perfect parents for me, especially given subsequent events in my life. The discipline I learned was wonderfully helpful in my schooling, in finding mentors, and even in finding my first employers (all of them used disciplined structures that I easily incorporated). I'm glad my formative years were with my parents in their earlier phase. And if I'd been the youngest, that would've been good too.

When we judge the past based on new learning in our present, we suffer. In contrast, we can value the roles of the past and appreciate the rich experience of growth.

Indefinite Cause and Effect

Lastly, I've discovered my concepts of cause and effect were limited by my understanding of time.

Example: Why Did I Divorce

For example, when my husband and I divorced, I had my list of reasons (mostly "his" short-comings) that supposedly "caused" my divorce. A year later, I'd done several workshops and recognized that many of my own short-comings were perhaps main contributing factors to the divorce—my list of "causes" for our divorce had changed. Many years later as our lives went in different directions, it became clear that the long-term directions of our lives wouldn't have been compatible. We'd seen buds of these differences before our divorce, so perhaps it was a subconscious knowing about our diverging future trajectories that was the "cause" of our divorce. Then, later, when I met my current husband, Daniel, I could see how my first marriage was the perfect training ground to fully appreciate Daniel. Daniel and I have been a perfect match both in supporting each other's growth and in enjoying coming together in multiple areas of life. However, Daniel and I wouldn't have been a match in our younger years. My first marriage was an essential first step to prepare me for my

second. Did an inner orchestration time my first marriage as well as its divorce?

Despite our similarities, at one point Daniel and I came
to what felt like an "irreconcilable difference" in what we
wanted in a relationship. Given my previous learning, I decided to hold the difference with curiosity and openness,
waiting to see what would unfold; I didn't know how the
difference between us would play out. Over the course of
the subsequent year, I grew into new preferences that I
wouldn't have expected and that aligned me with Daniel's
preference.

My models of cause and effect were an attempt to predict and control events of my life, but the models were
limited. When I relied exclusively on my ideas of cause
and effect, I attached to what I believed would lead to a
"good" future, and when reality didn't follow my preferences, I was disappointed or angry, certain that negative outcomes would follow. Fortunately, reality hasn't followed
my storyline for a "good" future–it's turned out much better than I could've planned. Life has surprised me over
and over, and disappointment has turned into gratitude.

To help loosen the ideas of cause and effect, consider this example of how the future pulls events toward itself even more than the past determines events ahead
of itself. Imagine somebody hard at work in the office at
7:30 pm on Friday evening who feels happy and excited

because she knows that she and her partner leave for her favorite vacation spot the next morning. Likewise imagine the same person sitting on a beautiful serene beach nine days later who feels dread because she knows that they leave shortly to return home and go to work the next morning. Next suppose she gets a message that she'll be given a long-awaited raise and promotion the next morning.

We don't know what the future holds. What may look like an imminent problem may not happen or may turn out to be a blessing. When we feel certain about our ideas of future outcomes, we tend to worry, blame, control and judge before we actually see what happens. On the other hand, when we remain open, curious, and available to the mystery of the moment-by-moment unfolding, we're freed from past regrets and future anxieties. Instead we become present to what is here now, free to flow with the unfolding, finding more creative options in the process. By releasing our certainty about causes and effects, we open to discovery.

In summary, time is merely a tool we use to structure our thoughts. We can use this tool in ways that are painful or ways that are curious and light. In honest contemplation, we have to admit that we don't know the best past or future. As we open to not knowing, we may find surprising gifts scattered throughout our lives and discover the grace already present right now.

Three ways to return to openness, discovery, and greater intimacy with true Being are to

1. **Identify a problem. Reframe it as a process. Consider that it's premature to make a judgment without more time.**

2. **Identify a regret. Notice the greater wisdom you now have. Identify blessings, insight, etc., that came from the experience that you regret. Would you give up that experience if you had to lose all the blessings and insights that also came with it?**

3. **Identify a current problem or past disappointment. Consider all the effects that you expect (or expected) as a result of that problem (or disappointment). Are you absolutely certain that this problem won't yield unexpected benefits and blessings? Or that the disappointment hasn't yielded unexpected benefits and blessings?**

4. **Are you willing to remain in the unknown regarding the outcome of things that appear as problems?**

Questions:

1. List three past problems that resolved themselves without the suffering you expected. [e.g., (1) My internet service was bad for the first three weeks of my new work-from-home job; it worked out just fine! (2) The guy who was supposed to fix our camper arrived drunk and left, but we ended up being able to fix it ourselves. (3) My friend got kicked out of his apartment and was homeless but found a new living situation and was fully supported through the process.]

_____

_____

_____

_____

2. List three blessings that came from a past problem you had. [e.g., fixing the camper ourselves was a fun project that endeared the camper to us even

more, saved us money, and helped us get to know more handyman resources in our town.]

_____

_____

_____

_____

3. Name a regret you have. [e.g., I sold my car to someone who could only pay with a payment plan and didn't make all the payments]

_____

_____

_____

_____

4. Consider that you did the best you could with the understanding you actually had (not that you thought you had) at that moment. [e.g., I was naive and trusting and really didn't know not to trust him]

_____

_____

_____

_____

5. What blessings or growth or new abilities or new relationships resulted from what happened? Can you absolutely know that what you regret shouldn't have happened? [e.g., I never severed the friendship and accepted that he couldn't make the payments; it was not a question for me to do anything else; I didn't know just how easily I prioritized friendship over money; in fact, it turned out to be a very generous thing I did without thinking and I can appreciate myself for that!]

_____

_____

_____

_____

6. Identify a disappointment in your life. [e.g., my mentor died young and left me.]

_____

_____

_____

_____

7. Did anything come out of that experience that you didn't predict? [e.g., I had to learn to listen to my own inner wisdom.]

_____

_____

_____

_____

8. How has your life ultimately benefitted from that situation beyond what you planned? [e.g., I've seen so many people rely on external authorities

and teachers and end up misguided; I've avoided that as my inner knowing has become very strong.]

---

9. Are you willing to consider that there may be a benevolence coordinating life better than you can plan? Are you willing to consider that you don't know the end of the story in situations that seem outside your preferences? [e.g., so far, every situation I thoroughly consider has brought good into my life; I'm willing to have the perspective that each new situation that arises will do the same.]

17:

Technique 15 Inestimable Importance

Everything in this physical world passes away. We eventually forget great inventors and their inventions and social leaders and their movements when they're replaced by newer advancements. True Being, nevertheless, persists timelessly as the vibrancy ringing through everything. True Being is the source of connection, fulfillment, and meaning. Once I experienced the profound fulfillment derived from being as opposed to doing, I also saw that the many forms of doing are all equally valuable because at their root they flow from the same core of Being despite their many different forms. The angry driver teaches me just like the peaceful sage teaches me. It's all one flow, one discovery.

Example: People in a Hospital Lobby

One afternoon I sat watching people in a hospital lobby. Some shared a moment with a loved one. Some were impatient. Some were absorbed in their devices. A pond of humanity. And there before me was the magical balance that exists in every moment, over and over and over again. There is the need and the service, the noticing and the being noticed, the problems and the problem solving, the boredom and entertainment, the strife and the resolution, the confusion and the systemization, etc. Every second a new mosaic of Being dancing with itself–each intricately balanced, finished and complete. No need for another moment. And yet another comes. What grace!

When I let Being have its role as the source of meaning and value rather than my own efforts, something in me shifts. I stop pushing and notice the aliveness already coursing through me. I notice that seeing, hearing, and even loving all occur before I make anything happen.

Example: A Pinch Off the Divine

I had the vision one day of something huge and brilliant as the sun pinching off a tiny bit of itself, purposefully including a particular concoction of its own traits. Then, it flicked the little bit into life as a human, exclaiming in pure joy, "I wonder what this one will do!" The sun-like being expected the human to have adventures of any kind, all equally fascinating. The main determining factor was simply the unique blend of traits that had been pinched off. The purpose of the human was simply to play out being herself.

As the expression of Being, I and you are inestimably precious exactly as our own concoction of humanness and timelessness. Our unique interests and experiences emanate from and return to true Being and can't go wrong.

Our value is beyond any reckoning that our minds could make. Being takes infinite interest in each moment of our lives; whether bored or suffering, mundane or exuberant, delighted or peaceful, each moment is the outflow of Being itself. We are the receivers of love and the givers of love. We are the savoring instruments of Being. If we saw ourselves fully, we'd drop to our knees in awe.

Each moment, like a rich wine, has its multiple notes, compounding to a now that will never be replaced again. To put it another way, as Being morphs through each new expression in each moment, it flows through masterpiece after masterpiece—each a unique composition of life, love, death, pain, and mystery. Your part and my part are absolutely essential for the masterpiece now. And now. And now.

Experiencing Being as the source of meaning, I see what in my life is unnecessary. I don't need my manager to know that it was my idea that enabled us to serve our higher number of clients today. I don't give a second thought to what car I'm driving when I give my esteemed friend a ride. I don't mind that I'm the one washing the dishes instead of being up front. Neither do I worry if I'm on the stage, uncertain if I have anything important to say. I'm free to sit and do nothing, to serve whatever need arises, to make the most grand discovery and never get the credit. Regardless of the circumstances, I'm full. I'm delighted with the preciousness of life itself.

The practice here is to

---

1. **Allow yourself to marinate in the experience of true Being as the source of meaning and preciousness.**
2. **Look at the efforting in your life and see what is overdone? What concerns are unnecessary?**
3. **If you had nothing to prove and nothing to avoid, what would you be free to do?**
4. **Experiment with engaging more with what enlivens you and less with everything else.**

Questions:

1. If you knew that this moment you're living in was the perfect orchestration of a master, how would you experience this moment differently? [e.g., I'd be okay that I had to apologize a third time to my partner for my impatience; I'd also be okay that our car has to get repaired yet again.]

_____

_____

_____

_____

2. If you knew that your very essence was golden, specifically chosen, an absolute success per the great design and that you could never mess up, what would change for you? [e.g., I'd see my apologies as opportunities for sweet connection rather

than errors; I wouldn't care if we postpone painting our house or if my child screamed in the store; I'd see it all as life's wonder.]

_____

_____

_____

_____

3. What word or phrase could remind you of your pre-ciousness, independent of (and completely includ-ing) anything you do? [e.g., Being is what lasts. I am golden. I can't help but be the diamond.]

_____

_____

_____

_____

4. Can you find a willingness to open to the possibility of the infinite value of Being in you? [e.g., yes, it feels more light and therefore probably more true.]

_____

_____

_____

_____

5. What beliefs to the contrary come up for you? Can you find a willingness to question these beliefs? [e.g., I have the belief that my child is unemployed because of my mistakes; questioning it, I discover that it's okay that my child is unemployed; I can be present and know that his unemployment is not just alright, but a perfect design; the highest purpose for his life requires him to go through the period of unemployment right now; in fact many great people went through long periods of unemployment.]

_____

_____

_____

_____

6. Look at the efforting in your life. What is over done? What concerns are unnecessary? [e.g., I was considering taking on a research project to help smooth over the relationship between my superior and a respected specialist even though it would have no real impact; I'm going to turn it down for something more meaningful to me]

_____

_____

_____

_____

7. If you had nothing to prove and nothing to avoid, what would you be free to do? [e.g., I'd turn down some social events to take time for painting with my acrylics with no concern about how it comes out; when at social events, I'd ask people about their passions rather than making small talk]

_____

_____

_____

_____

8. Experiment with engaging more with what enlivens you and less with everything else. [e.g., I told all the project managers at work that I'll only be attending the first 30 minutes of the meetings, saving a lot of energy and time]

_____

_____

_____

_____

18:

Technique 16 All the Facets

When we've experienced the fulfillment and joy of intimacy with true Being, we often hope for a repeat experience. With each meditation or spiritual practice, we may attempt to return to the already known and might use our past as a measuring stick against which we measure new experiences.

Example: The Bliss Trap

When I daily expected joy and lightness from my spiritual practice, every practice session felt so dull! I felt isolated from the wonder I knew was just beyond the veil. Mostly I felt numb and cold and sometimes exasperated. Then, one time I noticed that the emptiness might be worth investigating. I tuned into the emptiness and found that in the silence was an awesome immensity. I probed the vastness and found no edges, no limits. I opened to this infinity of space. It was nothing, absolute, unchanging. I discovered a new experience of expansiveness. My perception then dimmed again. However, I curiously continued to probe. I saw how my demands were minuscule in comparison with this infinity. How lucky I was even to exist and to perceive the mere surface of the greatness. It was everlasting in every conceivable way. Awe flowed over and through me. Rather than the same experience of joy that I'd had before, a new aspect of true Being was revealing itself. The grace overwhelmed me.

My yearning for the repeat experience came again during another practice session. This time I wondered if maybe true Being was there showing me yet another of its facets. I sat in the not-knowing, remaining curious despite the apparent dullness. Regardless of my experience through the session, I kept returning to the curious openness. Then I noticed how the dullness was soft and seemed to surround me entirely. I probed this softness and found that it seemed to be an ever-present enveloping essence. It wasn't exuberant or blissful, but it was gentle, undemanding, and constant. Could this softness be love in its most gentle of forms? Could love be so tender as to be a cottony blanket, an everyday presence that I regularly overlooked? I opened to the softness, dropping my expectations. As I became more still and available, the softness became more intense and full. I released my preferences and received its embrace. I couldn't name it, but gracious gentleness was its dominant characteristic. Tears flowed; it was fathomless in its mystery. Another facet of true Being had revealed itself to me.

Over the course of the subsequent weeks, the process repeated itself over and over. I experienced true Being as dynamic one day, as peace-exuding another day, as majestic another day, and so on. My appetite to repeat the same experience over and over was too small for true Being. Releasing my expectations, I opened more and more, and started to apprehend its infinite facets. I was no longer pursuing a known entity; I was in a discovery process with full emptiness.

This practice is to

---

1. **When Being feels distant, identify your expectations specifically.**
2. **Be willing that Being might appear differently than you expect.**
3. **Notice the subtleties of what is here and deepen your focus by describing it.**
4. **Relax fully into the subtlety of what is here, letting it be exactly what it is.**

Questions:

1. Have you had any peak experience that has become your benchmark? What aspect of true Being
   predominated in that experience? [e.g., I was joyful
   and light]

   _____

   _____

   _____

   _____

2. Are you absolutely certain that true Being has no
   other facets that might be equally or more interesting? [e.g., "joyful and light" would be too small a
   box for true Being]

   _____

   _____

   _____

   _____

3. Are you willing to be shown other aspects of true Being regardless of how it compares to your peak experience? [e.g., yes, fathomless mystery probably has infinite revelations]

_____

_____

_____

_____

4. Can you find a curious part of yourself that is interested in the infinite facets of true Being? What can you say to affirm flowing with this interest? [e.g., I open to experiencing unknown facets of true Being.]

_____

_____

_____

_____

5. Can you notice something already here beyond any effort? [e.g., silence is bathing everything]

_____

_____

_____

_____

6. Can you elaborate more on what is already here? [e.g., the silence is simultaneously weightless and potent]

_____

_____

_____

_____

7. Relax into the fullness of what is already here. [e.g.,
   I feel enfolded by the infinite holding of silence]

_____

_____

_____

_____

19:

Technique 17 Paradise

O ne night I had a dream of paradise. In this place, we never got what we asked for; instead we always got something better. If we went to a restaurant, they wouldn't bring us what we'd ordered but something we'd like better (according to our individual preferences). They might even close the restaurant and move us to a better one. If we went to a drug store, it might suddenly change to something better, like a flying carpet experience. In the center was a big hotel where they tried to give people only what they asked for as best they could. Interestingly, most people chose to stay in the hotel and take only short excursions out into paradise even though everyone was welcome to live at no cost in paradise.

Example: A Dull Moment at Work

After this dream, I started an experiment. Could it be true that each moment I'm actually in paradise without knowing it because I'm focusing on my ideas of what I want?

This experimental week transformed my thinking. For example, I was sitting at work in between patients. I had my book and no work to do at the moment. I asked myself how this moment could be paradise. I tuned into my body, and the vibration of life flowing effortlessly through me felt delicious! I looked at the colors of things around me, so many hues and shades, and noticed how some of them, a soft teal in particular, were a delight to behold. I heard the sounds from down the hall, people engaging with each other, clearly all caring and interested in their experience, whether joy or pain. I heard the mechanical sounds in my department, a fascinating modern symphony of whirs and rumbles. It started to feel like an amazing miracle that I should be sitting in a climate-controlled room, on a comfortable chair (oodles of inventions to create just these things) in the middle of a buzzing sea of humanity organizing itself toward numerous goals. Wonder spread through me at the countless expressions of life enveloping me as I sat as pure savoring awareness. Yes, each moment is paradise.

The thought-based identity has an appetite that is never filled. Its endless habit is to imagine what more could be added to make our experience better. In imagining something else, we stop fully experiencing what is. Not only do we miss out, our detachment pulls us out of the nurturing and grounding we naturally experience when we're fully present and imagines a vacancy that depletes our energy. For example, we might imagine our current circumstances but with another person added or with an improved version of ourselves or with a better setting or any number of conceptual improvements. We detach from the apparently "mundane" and retreat into a fantasy, missing the joy already present as we abandon the vibrancy of what is real for the illusion of what is only imagined, focusing on hopes rather than on what is given. We miss paradise because we never fully investigate it.

As this experiment has become my way of life, I've discovered the sensuousness of each moment. Each person I meet has interesting tones to their voice. The multiple light sources around me have varying directions and hues causing a unique blend of illumination, sparkling reflection, and shadow. So many gadgets abound at every turn, each offering one convenience or another. And the eyes of every person I meet have their own depth, their own being, their own life emanating through them. What endless wonder!

All it takes to discover paradise is to drop the assumption that this moment isn't it and become willing to investigate what is already here.

This practice is to

---

1. **When reality seems inadequate, identify what unavailable option you're fixating on.**
2. **Look to see what is actually here already, paying special attention to your senses.**
3. **With curiosity, look further to notice the support constantly flowing toward you in the moment.**
4. **If you were told that this moment is a paradise custom-made for you, what more would you notice?**

Questions:

1. What is the common theme in any paradise you imagine? For example, it might be ideal weather, absence of work, better relationships, etc. [e.g., being on vacation]

---

2. Can you find a willingness to see a paradise different than your own mental creation? [e.g., yes, maybe a working life is paradise too]

_____

_____

_____

_____

3. Look at where you are right now. What sensations are in your body? How do you know you're alive? What sounds do you hear? What tones do they have? What colors are around you? How do they vary? What light and shadow is around you? Are you making your heart beat or your cells absorb nutrients or your senses perceive? What is there to be grateful for? What is there to cherish? [e.g., my vocation has enjoyable moments of using my skills, I'm appreciated at times for what I do, my vocation

gives me perspectives from people that I wouldn't get any other way, I've had a lot of fun honing my skills, I like the quiet rooms where I work]

---

4. If you were told that this moment had been perfectly customized for you, what would you notice and appreciate? [e.g., the sunlight in my room is particularly nice, I have a great boss, there is a wonderful blend of creativity and logic in what I do, I get to wear comfortable clothing at work, I get paid more than I need for my work]

20:

Technique 18 Sacrifice versus Joy of Loving

I can't count how many times I've been unhappy about a situation, and ultimately, the solution was to celebrate the abundant love flowing through me toward another person. I've now come to see that cultivating our ability to enjoy our own loving nature is a great challenge to our thought-based identity. Here is a simple example:

Example: A Caring Moment With My Partner Made Me Late

I was on the way out the door to an event when my partner asked for some help. I didn't want to be late, but I also saw my partner's need and wanted to help, so I took a few minutes to help him. Then, I left for the event. On the way there, I noticed the time and was disappointed that I was likely to be late.

Since I was disappointed, I looked for my "should-be" ideas so I could inquire into them. Clearly, I thought I should be on time. And, every time that thought went through me, I felt my gut tighten up. I opened to the possibility that maybe it was all perfect. How could that be? What was good about my situation?

It took longer than normal to recognize the hidden blessing—I'd shared a loving moment helping my partner. The moment had been very simple, but it symbolized the priority he and I placed on our relationship, the trust and support we shared, and the natural love that motivated us. This relationship was one of the most important parts of my life, and yet my instinct was to overlook or minimize the little moments that built the relationship and focus on my tardiness. I knew that within a month, what time I arrived to the event would not even cross my mind. But, I would continue to cherish my relationship. In simple moments like these, we nurtured our relationship, and our relationship was incalculably important to me.

We habitually take for granted our everyday open-hearted acts of care instead of relishing the way love flows through us, often without us even thinking about it. Yet, what could be more important in life?

Example: Parents Up At Night With Their Childen

I've noticed this pattern over and over. Parents get up for hours at night to take care of a sick child, and then they feel dismal starting their day. Thoughts flood in about their fatigue and their busy day ahead. They chalk up their experience to the "sacrifices of parenthood" and might even momentarily envy the freedom of their childless co-workers. Love happened that night. Sure, there may have been cranky moments, tears, and impatience, but love's certainty underlay all the tension. The parent and the child share a certainty that the parent will be there for the child, period. The challenges of the night couldn't scratch the undercurrent of love, support, commitment, and secure care between the parent and the child.

When we freely love another person, our thought-based identity belittles the experience by turning our focus to the costs to us. Our thought-based identity can't take the credit for spontaneous loving responses, which are evidence instead of the naturally loving nature of life flowing through us. When we cherish this natural flow of love, we actually diminish the stance of control and effort required by our thought-based identity. So, our thought-based identity downplays our natural virtues by reframing them as sacrifices. For example, the art teacher regrets the time lost for the development of his own craft, minimizing the many years of mentoring youth through important life situations.

The practice here is to

---

1. **Identify an ongoing frustration you have in regards to another person or a sacrifice you make for someone else.**
2. **Identify how loving them is influencing the way you're handling the situation.**
3. **Can you pause to appreciate the love you share?**
4. **Reflecting on the value of love as an outflow of true Being, can you open more fully to true Being as you acknowledge the love flowing through you?**

When we pause, reflect, and cherish our moments of loving generosity, we connect more palpably with true Being and with the natural ways love and kindness flow through us with little thought. As we change our focus and allow ourselves the rich enjoyment of our loving nature, our hearts soften. We notice the natural generosity of ourselves and then of others as well. We are more tuned in to the fundamental care expressing itself naturally in every day moments.

Questions:

1. Can you remember a sacrifice you made recently for someone you care about or a frustration you have with someone else? What did you give up? [e.g., I vacationed with my family in a place much more congested and less beautiful than where I live; I had a house guest who kept repeating complaints about her boyfriend]

_____

_____

_____

_____

2. What did this situation demonstrate about the blessings in this relationship long-term? [e.g., we value each other's presence and simply being together; I have seen my house guest grow a lot over time and am glad I support her]

_____

_____

_____

_____

3. Are you willing to fully acknowledge the loving aspects of this situation? Do you notice any tendency in yourself to find your mistakes and minimize the love? [e.g., I tend to think how I wasn't as happy on the vacation as I am at home but there's no merit in making such comparisons--it was a loving time together, playful and appreciative--I was happy to meet up with them; I feel a natural urge to be a support in my house guest's life--she's important to me]

_____

_____

_____

_____

4. How would you describe the underlying loving nature expressing itself in that situation? [e.g., I naturally took the trip because I love them and they love me--that simple action demonstrates the connection that is such a precious part of life; my

guest's ongoing process of discovery may seem
slow but I enjoy her breakthroughs]

_____

_____

_____

_____

5. Take a moment to appreciate yourself, your loving
   nature, and the relationship important to you in this
   situation. [e.g., I enjoyed them without focusing on
   the congestion and enjoyed taking part in what they
   enjoyed--clearly, love was carrying me rather than
   my egoic preferences--I was naturally supporting
   our relating without even considering otherwise, a
   very sweet open-hearted way to be; it's grace to
   be a loving space for my guest's learning process]

_____

_____

_____

_____

21:

Technique 19 Welcoming Diminishment

Perhaps one of the most challenging but impactful approaches to dismantling our thought-based identities is to spend time with people who appear antagonistic, demeaning, combative, or critical. These situations typically push our buttons (our psychological triggers), blatantly outlining the ideas we want others to have about us but don't. We recognize which apparent offenses bother us the most and use them to identify the ideations of our thought-based identity. We see ourselves one way and someone else sees us another way, and it particularly irritates us when they miss the traits we consider important in our thought-based identity. Once we recognize these identifications, we surrender them as we practice nonresistance to being everything.

Example: The Criticized Intern

Here's an example. I was interning with a company where my assignment one day was to work with a team member who started criticizing me in the morning and continued into the afternoon. With each criticism, I noticed the part of me that wanted to be acknowledged for my strengths and then surrendered this desire instead, opening to the possibility that I might yet have much to learn. With each new criticism, I looked to see if there was any helpful input for me to remember. Sometimes I saw that I had been absent-minded, and other times I saw that it was a new training point I didn't remember receiving before. I took note of each point, simply being a student with nothing to prove. At one point, she said with obvious irritation, "What is it with you today?" After having done the above exercise all day long with her criticism, I smiled easily and said, "Yes, I seem out of it today, I'm sorry." I felt no resistance, and her words flowed right through my space, in and out. I felt less solid than usual and felt compassion that she was obviously unhappy that day. I, on the other hand, felt especially light as the whole experience had called me into presence all day long.

Once we don't have an identity to defend, we become as fluid as the universe. Looking at our lives, we see that at different times we've been truthful and we've been false, we've been wise and we've been foolish, we've been kind and we've been unkind.

I consider the ocean to be my teacher. It can be gentle and terrible and everything in between. And all of its forms have been a perfect wonder of teaching and comforting, pushing and supporting. I am no greater than the ocean. To be all of it doesn't mean that I don't apologize. When I see a desire to express more kindness than I have, I apologize because it's congruent with the natural desire in myself to be kind. I value kindness and other virtues deeply—not because they fit with my thought-based identity and make me look good, but because they are consistent with my natural deepest desires. They feel most aligned with what brings me joy and lightness.

Since my thought-based identity believes it's essential that I'm helpful and kind, people who consider me hostile or selfishly motivated have all triggered my identity into reactivity, which is hitting pay dirt in the mining of my mental ideations underlying my thought-based identity.

Rather than defending, I've learned to jump at the opportunity to unravel that which pulls me out of true Being where I'm serenely nothing and have no investment in other people's ideas about me. I've learned that what causes the offense is the other person not agreeing with the ideas I want them to believe. My moment of defensiveness points out a belief that I might not have recognized. This idea about myself is a brick in the structure of my thought-based identity. I didn't even recognize my self-concept until the offense happened and I felt the rigidity of my assumptions about myself. When I unravel this belief, I discover a previously hidden path back to true Being.

Usually the opportunity is two-fold. Before someone attacks my ideas about myself (which are my triggers), there's often a moment when I've subtly pulled away from them. Rarely does someone push my button without me having done something first (maybe very minor and possibly misunderstood). So first I sit with the offense and look for any moment where I subtly disturbed the relationship. I may have compared myself to them or operated from a place of authority or withdrawn support or challenged them in some small way without even noticing it.

Next I look at their offensive comment and identify the idea I have about myself that was challenged. Do I consider myself kinder than they implied? Or wiser? Or more competent? Or more _____ (fill in the blank)? Now I've struck gold. If I maintain this idea about myself (or any idea for that matter), I pull myself out of the full experience of true Being. Next I identify the opposite position, for example "kind" might become "self-serving," "intelligent" might become "naive," and "competent" might become "careless." Then I ask myself if I'm willing to see myself as both, e.g., "kind" *and* "self-serving." When I can see myself as all of it, the "should-be" ideas of rigid identification lose their grip, and I relax into the All, into the nothingness of true Being.

Lastly I apologize to the other person without defending, preferably in person but at least in spirit. As I do so, I often feel a sinking sensation inside me, sometimes even gut-wrenching—not a pleasant sensation! My thought-based identity feels dismissed, used, and sad. But this discomfort is the cloud that yields the rainbow, so I notice the egoic pain and hold it in a compassionate embrace.

As my goals and preferences align more with the priority of experiencing myself as true Being, the sensations of diminishment pass more and more quickly and have new interpretations. I feel vulnerable, hollow, and less solid, almost trembling inside, and this diminishment of the thought-based identity is exactly what I want—it opens me to true Being!

Example: A Demand for Apology

As another example, a close friend demanded an apology for an act I'd considered courageous and supportive (mentioning a counselor to her that specialized in her situation). She specified that the apology include a statement that what I'd done was completely inappropriate and uncalled for. It turned out that she hadn't wanted my help and saw the act as hostile and condescending. In this case, to apologize to her seemed to validate her interpretation of my aggression. I sat with this situation for a long time before I could see her point—I'd undermined her competence by rushing in with my help. When I wrote my apology, I felt two parts inside me. The first knew what was called of me and flowed into doing it. The other part felt diminished, hollow, vulnerable, and anxious that this apology would be twisted and used to substantiate future criticism. As I stilled myself, I recognized my thought-based identity feeling threatened and then felt a rush of gratitude. I clearly was apologizing from a selfless place and could see how my thought-based identity prioritized its own self-protection. In being seen, the thought-based identity became less substantial. I didn't feel comfortable, but I was exactly aligned with my truest goals. I spontaneously closed my written apology with a heartfelt thank you and sent it to her.

Example: Apologizing to My Husband

As a last example, I said something unkind to my husband, and my own criticism popped up that I should be a kinder person. The "should" idea was distinct from the part of me that wanted to go immediately and make it right. Instead, this criticism focused on *me* and how I should be more open-hearted, more appreciative, etc. I hadn't lived up to my thought-based identity. I noticed the suffering (guilt) resulting from these beliefs and felt the corresponding tightness in my chest. While believing "I should be kind," I found it difficult to confront the moment and apologize to my husband; rather, feeling guilty, I wanted to defend or blame! I noticed the opportunity for diminishment. I wasn't the kind, loving person of my mentally constructed identity. I was fluid, taking every form. Sitting with this realization, the guilt changed to humility. I put the beliefs aside and went and apologized. He very sweetly appreciated my apology and even gave a reason for why I might have said what I said. Clearly he still loved me. In fact, I felt his love even more intensely in his response to me! My "failing" was actually an opportunity for love if I would only drop my beliefs and focus on what was actually there— his lovingkindness and my own desire to reconnect. If there was any diminishment of love, it was in the way my self-criticism constricted my heart and made me want to pull away from him. Reality, as I opened to it, was full of love. Seeing his love, I could be the "one who is loved and forgiven," rather than the "one who must always be kind." Reality was a very happy place to be.

The practice here is to

---

1. **Identify a moment you were criticized that triggered you.**
2. **Find the idea you hold about yourself that was challenged.**
3. **Consider that you might be both that idea and its opposite.**
4. **Look to see if you subtly pulled away from the person before the offense happened.**
5. **See if you are willing to have your thought-based identity diminished.**
6. **Prepare an apology (and deliver it if appropriate) for wherever you feel an intention for better relating.**

The moment we feel defensive we follow the pointer to our thought-based identity. In stillness and presence, we uncover its ruse and surrender into the freedom of true Being.

Questions:

1. Identify a time when you were offended. Recall the specific circumstances. [e.g., my neighbors told me the third time how to water my flowers better]

_____

_____

_____

_____

2. Now look at the offensive comment made to you. What aspect of yourself did it challenge? Your authority? Your wisdom? Your kindness? Etc. [e.g., they seem to think my yard is a sore spot to their eyes; I think of myself as someone who keeps up her property responsibly and with some taste]

_____

_____

_____

_____

3. What is the opposite of the above trait? [e.g., I'm negligent of my property]

_____

_____

_____

_____

4. Can you open to seeing yourself as *both*? Sometimes "right" and sometimes "wrong"? Notice the sensations of any resistance and anything else that arises. [e.g., yes, I'm certainly not in line for top gardener and I like a more "natural" wild look then a manicured look; I'm probably neglectful by their standards]

_____

_____

_____

_____

5. Can you open to your nothingness? To being the All? [e.g, it's completely relative--I'm both tasteful and negligent; I'm all of it]

_____

_____

_____

_____

6. Now look for a moment before the offense when you did something that subtly asserted your superiority or subtly withdrew from the other person. (It might've been something that was misunderstood.) [e.g., we moved in to a home that used to be owned by a hobby gardener on a prominent corner that might have been the pride of the neighborhood and haven't kept up her style]

_____

_____

_____

_____

7. Consider how this moment may have impacted the other person. [e.g., they probably feel a loss in the appearance and maybe even value of the neighborhood]

_____

_____

_____

_____

8. Now write (and consider sharing) an apology to the person. [e.g., I can hear their concern with under-standing with no defensiveness]

_____

_____

_____

_____

22:

Technique 20 Byron Katie's Worksheet

For me Byron Katie Michell's *Judge Your Neighbor Worksheet* is the gold-standard process for seeing through the "should-be" ideas of our elusive thought-based identity. The worksheet is designed to expose an aspect of this identity and use it to bring us to freedom.

Any time we tense up, get upset, feel hurt or sad, or even feel indecisive, this worksheet brings clarity to the falsehood of the assumptions underlying our thought-based identity and guides us to the point where our beliefs become unconvincing and drop away, seemingly of their own accord.

The worksheet is not a mental process. It uses questions, but the answers come from feeling into our bodies and emotions and meditatively waiting for inner clarity. I don't consider a worksheet finished until I feel the "should-be" idea drop away and my body and heart open in a fresh "Aha!" of freedom.

You can find the free worksheet at www.thework.com. And you can also see instructions there for how to use it as well as YouTube examples. I've included the worksheet with full instructions in the appendix. Here I'm going to describe how a worksheet works for me with the following example.

Example: Bad Grade on My Exam

I received a barely passing grade on an exam at school—I was back in school for a career change. I'd studied for the exam but had focused on material that turned out to be less relevant. My grade didn't fit with my plan of doing so well that my performance would speak for itself and allow me to easily get a job in a distant job market. I felt the grade was undeserved, and, worse yet, it seemed to threaten my plans. I was anxious about my situation, disappointed in myself, and angry that the instructor had been so vague! So, I did a worksheet. (I always write them on paper because the more pointed focus yields a more powerful "Aha!")

There are two parts to the process: (1) to answer the questions that elaborate my complaint and then (2) to question all my answers. When sitting down to answer the questions of a worksheet, I only embody the part of me that is upset. The point of the worksheet is to unravel a specific thinking pattern, so bouncing between perspectives doesn't work. In fact the instructions are to identify a specific moment when the upset dominated my awareness and to do the whole worksheet from my perspective in that moment. Without this focus, I'd write an ineffective worksheet that didn't clearly represent the egoic belief. Even if the upset doesn't entirely feel authentic anymore, I stay in the upset because, given that the upset hasn't completely dropped away, the underlying belief is worth examining. I complete the worksheet entirely from the perspective of the upset, even slightly exaggerating it to get at its core and not tempering it in any way.

Also I don't skip any parts as I fill out the worksheet because it's designed to unearth many facets of the upset. The most obvious aspect may not be the actual crux of the matter. So I don't leave any blanks. The first question asks for my emotions and for the situation. In my example, "I was anxious and angry because I got a 76% on my test." Notice how I narrowed it down to a few specific emotions and to a single main issue.

The second question starts to flesh out my preferences–my ideas of what would be better. Continuing with my example, "I wanted to excel at the test and ensure my employability in another state."

The third question taps into the part of me that wants to play "God." It asks me to list the advice I'd give in the situation. Here it's important not to speak in generalizations (for example, I should get a good grade), but instead to be as specific as possible in naming the specific behaviors we'd prescribe and their timing. So in my example "I should've known which topics were more important, and I should've studied even more by not getting together with friends." (Notice I was specific about when I should've changed my activity to studying.)

The fourth part taps into the most impassioned part of this identified part of myself. I don't hold back. It asks what is needed for me to be happy. Again, specificity helps. "I want a top 10% grade; I want understanding of the priorities in this field; I want easy time-management and memory-recall, and I want superiority over others." Given that I was still in my first semester in a two-year program, I had to chuckle as I recognized my immature tantrum—I wanted it all figured out *now*.

The fifth question delves further into the nature of the identification by soliciting adjectives. How would I describe the disappointing culprit? Well, in my example (remembering to stay in the mindset of the upset) I considered myself to be at fault. "I am stupid, irresponsible, negligent, obtuse, and a smug slacker."

Finally the last question ties it all up nicely. What did I never want to experience again? In this case, "I never want to have poor performance nor find it difficult to get the employment I want."

Whew! I had finally elaborated the opinions of the identified part, and it felt good to have let it out.

Now I went through the unraveling process. I took each statement and asked the four questions at the bottom of the worksheet (the most important set of questions) and then turned the statements around.

The final four questions that unravel the thoughts laid out in the first set of questions are:

1. Is it true?
2. Can I absolutely know it is true?
3. How do I react and what happens when I believe that thought?
4. Who would I be without that thought?

Now let's look at my answer to the first question and how I applied the final four questions:

"Was it true that I'd performed poorly on the test?"

"Yes."

"Could I absolutely know I'd performed poorly on the test?"

"Yes."

"How do I feel when I believe that thought?"

"Guilty, anxious, dense, scared, mad, sad, and very constricted, tight and heavy."

"How would I feel if I didn't have that thought?" In other words, how would I feel if I were incapable of being disappointed in my performance?

"Well, I'd feel much lighter! It would be a circumstance to investigate with curiosity rather than a personal downfall. I wouldn't be so certain about what was needed and essential for things to work out. I'd be more relaxed and open."

Wow! Just feeling the difference was nice. I could see how my beliefs made the situation five times worse than the situation itself.

Finally it was time to turn the statement around. There are many ways to turn a statement around, such as reversing the subject and object of the verb (such as "he hates me" becomes "I hate him"), changing any word to one with an opposite meaning ("he hates me" becomes "he loves me"), merely adding a "not," etc. Here are the turnarounds that I found most helpful.

"I should've performed poorly on my test." Now the power of the turnaround is to sit as long as it takes to find three specific substantiating examples in real life that support the turnaround. (1) "It made me feel more kinship with other students especially those who were struggling."

(Here is an example of where the priorities of true Being might be different than my priorities.) (2) "It gave me a big alarm that I need to organize my life for more study time. Fortunately, I was recognizing the need for more study time early on before I took any final exams." (3) "It gave me more respect for the project I was undertaking, for myself in doing it, and for others already in the field. Becoming an expert was not going to be a walk in the park."

The insight just from these three substantiating examples was already very helpful! Clearly the situation wasn't all bad. Then I moved on to questioning the next statement.

"Was it true that I wanted to excel at my test and to ensure my employability?"

"Yes!"

"Could I absolutely know that to excel was what I wanted?"

After a moment's reflection, I was surprised to have to say, "No." Repeatedly in my life, I hadn't gotten my first choice and then later discovered that my second or third choice turned out to be better than the first choice. I had to admit that only much later when I can look back on a situation do I have enough clarity to see what really works best. My preferences in the midst of a situation often turn out to be misguided.

Next, "How do I feel when I believe that I want to excel at my test and ensure my employability?"

"Well, I noticed how the thought brought me back to being so certain about what is best for me, and with that thought came closed-mindedness with a palpable rigidness in my body and lots of tension."

"How would I feel without this thought?"

"I'd feel less burdened, less the 'master of my destiny' who had to try to control the uncontrollable." Spontaneously, I deeply exhaled as I felt tension draining from my body with this admission.

This process of tuning into the effects of demands and control in our being and then feeling the somatic effects of freedom repeats many times during the worksheet and gradually deepens the realizations of the whole worksheet, so it's valuable to do each part thoroughly every time.

Lastly I turned the statement around: "I don't want to excel at my test and find employment easily. "Wow! How was I going to find three pieces of substantiating evidence for that? It took some pondering. (1) "I was glad to have seen my friends and hadn't wanted to give that up. In fact, now as I expected to see my friends much less, I could feel that the decision wouldn't be so hard because I'd gotten this grade. Now I could see in black and white how I needed to manage my time! Rarely do I get messages with such clarity! Doing poorly on the test was a gift." (2) "This test still left me two more tests and my final! This clarity came early enough that it might not impact my GPA. If I needed this message, then now was the time." (3) "I like the greater respect I have for the field I'm entering. It would be more challenging than I thought, which for me meant it would be more interesting and enjoyable." The evidence was mounting that maybe the grade was part of a benevolent flow of events.

On to the next statement: "Was it true that I should've known what was more important in the course material and I should've studied even more by not getting together with friends?"

"No." I couldn't say that any of these "should's" were actually true.

"How did it make me feel to believe I should've known, etc.?

"There was the familiar tension as though I had to organize the world." Wow! I spent so much energy in trying to control what I couldn't control! My beliefs brought me so much constriction.

"How would I feel without this belief?"

"I'd be grateful for the time with my friends without regrets. I'd notice the novelty of doing poorly on a test.

There would even be a comedic element to find out I'd entered a more challenging field than I thought. Mostly I'd be curious as to how this drama would play out. It certainly made life interesting and drew my attention."

Lastly, the turnaround: "I shouldn't have known what was important in the test material and shouldn't have studied more." As I reflected, I still believed the opposite, but could I find substantiating evidence for this turnaround? (1) "I was learning a lot about how much tension I was living in as I tried to do it all; that was a big benefit in this inquiry." (2) "Focusing more completely on my studies would actually be an easier life. That was true." Okay, one more to go. (3) "If I needed to study more for the program, it was better to find out earlier with minimal negative consequences than to find out later. In this way it was a gift." And another came, too. (4) "It was true that I couldn't have known what the test would be like, and life was teaching me to be present along the way and flexibly make adjustments —to be responsive." In fact, that was a skill I wanted to build, and here was my chance! Something was working it all out for my benefit.

On to the next statement: "Was it true that I wanted a top 10% grade, superiority, easy memory-recall and time-management, and knowledge now about the priorities in this field?"

I had to answer, "No." My true priorities in life are what matters on one's deathbed—the strength of my relationships and time enjoying creativity, learning, and beauty. Having an easy time was not necessarily going to help me have my true priorities. The rightness of the whole situation was sinking in. I wanted personal growth and development, not an easy ride. Period. Wow! The opposite just arose inside me as an undeniable truth. I noticed the difference in my body between the original want list and my new awareness. How did I feel with and without the belief? I went from "feeling anxious and blind" to "feeling grounded, serene, competent and open." I wanted to abide in this serenity and openness. The turnaround was so obviously more true! I wanted connection to others, to being, and the ability to negotiate through challenges. I couldn't have designed a better wake-up call for myself. I was convinced. The knowing was so solid that I continued to the next statement without further turnarounds.

"Was it true that I was stupid, irresponsible, negligent, obtuse, and a smug slacker?"

"Yes, at times, " but it no longer mattered.

"Was it absolutely true?"

"No." As true Being, I include everything, all of these traits and their opposites.

"How did each of these beliefs make me feel?"

"I could feel the stubbornness of the original thought—it was so blind, closed-minded, and disconnected."

"How did I feel without the thought?"

"My new state of being felt wiser, more expanded, and gentle."

The turnaround was obvious. "It wasn't my performance that was stupid, irresponsible, etc.; rather, it was the judging mindset that was stupid, irresponsible, negligent, obtuse, and a smug slacker." How ironic that the thought-based identity that wanted so badly to be competent was actually so narrow-minded that it made itself ridiculous! "The mindset was stupid and irresponsible wanting an easy ride." I needed no further substantiations for something so obvious.

Moreover, I found another turnaround: "True Being was open and responsive and a quick learner in what really matters." These attributes were clear to me as this turnaround rang true in the depths of my being.

So, on to the final statement: "Was it true that I never wanted to have poor performance or have difficulty getting employment?"

"No."

"How did it make me feel to think that I never wanted poor performance or difficulty getting employment?"

"It made me feel like the world was dangerous."

"How did I feel without these beliefs?"

"I felt fluid, soft, less certain, and more connected to the flow of what is."

Could I turn the statement around? Yes. "I look forward to any time that I perform poorly or have difficulty finding employment. "Yes! Already this experience had taught me to simplify my life and to be curious and flexible instead of performance-driven. I welcome experiences such as these because they unravel my false sense of identity and carry me into true Being—nothing matters more. They open me to flexibility, to responsiveness, and to appreciation of what is.

The upset had dropped away, replaced by gratitude. And if the upset were to come back, I would only need to do another worksheet to unearth remaining aspects of my beliefs in this situation. Whenever I have to do multiple worksheets, each worksheet reveals additional insight and further dissolves my thought-based identity.

Of numerous practices I've tried, doing a Judge-Your-Neighbor worksheet is the gold-standard approach for revealing and undoing egoic beliefs. I even use worksheets when I'm indecisive by doing a worksheet from the position of each competing preference. When I feel tension or anxiety suddenly grip me, I simply identify the stray belief that brought about the tension and do a worksheet on that belief. When I feel myself using any compulsive behavior (which in my case could be rehearsing my to-do lists), I identify the triggering moment and put the thoughts of that moment into a worksheet.

Doing one worksheet a day for thirty days in a row has been as awakening as any spiritual retreat in which I've participated.

The practice here is the Judge-Your-Neighbor Worksheet, which is in the appendix or at thework.com.

Questions:

1. What is a regret or upset you currently have? [e.g., neighbors shouldn't be noisy late at night]

_____

_____

_____

_____

2. Pick a specific situation and moment in time that exemplifies this upset. [e.g., Friday night I didn't like hearing their conversations when i was in bed]

_____

_____

_____

_____

3. Embodying the mindset of your concerns and perspectives in that moment, fill out a Judge-Your-Neighbor Worksheet. [e.g.,, *I fill out a full worksheet; rather than sharing the whole worksheet here, I'm going to use my answer from question 3 for these questions*: my neighbors should take their conversations indoors after 9:00 pm and should use quieter voices outside]

_____

_____

_____

_____

4. Now take the first statement and ask each of the four questions—Is it true? and so on. [e.g., it's not true that my neighbors should be quieter at 9:00; I feel even more tense when I'm operating from this belief; without this thought I'm more relaxed and might stay up reading a while or might even fall asleep]

_____

_____

_____

_____

5. Now turnaround the statement to its opposite. Find three examples of how that opposite statement is true. [e.g., my neighbors should make noise--well yes, they are happily enjoying themselves and being alive expressive human beings--I much prefer that than a rigidly controlled society! And, they should feel comfortable in their own yard. And, I

hope they would grant me tolerance if I had friends over at night at some point.]

---

6. Make another turnaround of the statement to a different opposite. Find three examples of how that opposite statement is true. [e.g., I should be quieter--yes, my up-tight thinking should be quieter and give more room for flexibility, liveliness, and cheer. I should calm the extra tension I'm adding and find ways of enjoying the evening, perhaps listening to soft music. I should be quieter in the morning when I exuberantly take my morning walks and sometimes call to my husband while others are sleeping]

---

7. Continue with the above 4, 5, and 6 instructions with each of the next five statements on your Judge-Your-Neighbor worksheet.

_____

_____

_____

8. Now how do you feel? Have you reached a full release regarding the situation? If not, reclarify what really bothers you in the situation. Fill out another worksheet. Then ask the four questions and write the turnarounds. This process may take a few days. The freedom is worth the work! Don't settle for less than a full "Aha!" and freedom. [e.g. the voice wanting them to be quiet is a cranky old voice that doesn't reflect my real appreciation for liveliness and vitality and social sharing; I can enjoy them and celebrate their freedom!]

_____

_____

_____

23:

Conclusion

One of the greatest misunderstandings regarding knowing true Being is linking it to feeling happy and secure. When we're operating from the thought-based identity, we tend to alternate between unhappy and happy based on how the world aligns with the expectations of the thought-based identity. And, the two experiences (happy and unhappy) are actually quite alike because they are grounded in the ideas and preferences of our thinking. In this diagram, they are both boxes defined by the preferences made up in our thinking.

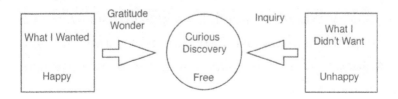

As an example of living in the "happy box," when we get the job or relationship we decided to be best for us, we feel happy. In our minds, our lives are going according to plan, but we've subtly inserted our evaluation between us and the intimate experience of reality. We've lost touch with the open freedom, curiosity, and wonder of true Being. Because we're evaluating life by what we want, we've returned to a reified self-concept and are living from the box of our concepts and expectations.

In contrast, when we live from true Being, we live fluidly with the mysterious, shown as a circle in the diagram. There is little definition and no need for particular circumstances. Of course, desires arise, and we move toward them, but we aren't attached to specific outcomes. We experience peace and freedom not because we get what we want or because we're continually "happy"; rather, because we know ourselves to be deeper than "happy" and "not happy." We know as a core certainty of experience the one benevolent flow of true Being.

The arrows show possible ways of moving back to freedom. When we're grateful and tune in to the wonder of our experience, we move from "happy" to "free." To move from "unhappy" to "free," we inquire with techniques such as those in this book.

Here's another example of how I moved from the "happy" to "free." I noticed that after we bought a great sunny house one mile from the ocean, I sometimes hoped we would live in the house the rest of my life ("happy"). And, this thought was actually painful compared to my normal free way of being--I could feel a constriction of attachment whenever I had this thought. So, after observing this tightness several times, it was too painful to bear, and I gave up the thought. Instead, I'm enjoying the house as long as I'm in it, and I don't know more than that ("free"). To live in the mystery is a much more open, light, free experience completely independent of plans and expectations. Now, I'm grateful moment-to-moment for today's experience in the house.

In this case, by simply noticing my internal state of constriction, I connected to that which prefers freedom. In fact, I've used careful, intentional noticing to propel me toward peace and freedom again and again. I don't have to try to motivate myself to use these techniques. When I carefully and intentionally notice the lightness of my experiences of freedom and peace and the heaviness of my experiences of attachment and evaluation, the desire arises to inquire into any illusion of trouble.

The thought-based identity considers certain situations to be "safe" or "secure" because the external world follows our preferences, such as health for our loved ones or income in excess of expenses, etc. However, we know that the thought-based identity is never safe or secure--it's always tenuous. The more we define happiness and security by our expectations, the more we're subject to anxiety, shame, and offense.

In contrast, true Being can't be threatened. The one benevolent flow is undiminishable and timeless. Situations come and go, but living as true Being, we are the indestructible essence that is unchanged by circumstances. The more we open to mystery, the easier it is to experience the peace and freedom of true Being.

What is the difference between an orchard and a forest? They look completely different, don't they? Orchards have ordered rows of similar trees; forests have a huge diversity of trees growing in a dance of forms and directions. Our ideas about how people and ourselves should be are so restrictive that, if they were followed, life would be much more like an orchard than like a forest.

Another example is a puzzle. Imagine we're all puzzle pieces. Now if everyone were fair and equally self-sufficient and always appropriate with each other, no piece would overlap into the space of another piece. No one would cross someone else's boundaries; no one would take too much from another, etc. There would be no inter-locking holes and arms. At most the pieces would have nice wavy lines. But what about the pieces with big holes gouged out of their sides or big fat arms extending into other pieces? The more complex puzzle more accurately reflects the nature of reality. The fullest human experience involves a plethora of give and take. When life brings surprises (e.g., a favorite co-worker gets randomly fired), I remind myself that we live in the more interesting puzzle and watch to see what good will come.

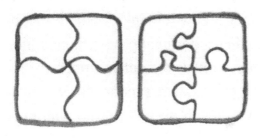

Our ideas about "living to our potential," "being self-sufficient," "equal opportunity," etc., don't reflect the life that is. Of course, the call of life often moves us toward such ideals. But, when we judge what is here now according to our ideals, we distance ourselves from the inherent beauty available to open hearts and minds. I learned so much from watching a homeless man in New York City--his fearlessness, his flexibility, his willingness to say what he felt--every person teaches me. The baby who lives mere weeks teaches me the sweetness of being and how little is needed for a complete life. One man that I deeply admire had parents that didn't even keep him fed as he grew up, yet with this he developed a character that has greatly impacted me. I have learned that jumping to conclusions is a recipe for suffering. Life is a continual discovery of enjoyment and infinite expression.

Life is our perfect workshop, exquisitely designed to rid us of illusion and bring us to fullness of life and love. My teacher is every person, every interaction, every situation. In fact, I now remember before this birth setting up my life to include among other things the opportunity to journey through restriction and then to rediscover freedom, an exhilarating experience and favorite adventure. I wanted to be on the playing field developing an ego (thought-based identity) and then dissolving it. The approaches here came from close observation of this dissolution. Without my ideations about how things should be different, I experience life as an endless gift and each moment as grace.

"Nothing real can be threatened; nothing unreal exists. Herein lies the peace of God." *A Course in Miracles*

"The only price of joy is giving up the right to make anything wrong." Lisa Carrillo

"Listen to your life. See it for the fathomless mystery it is. In the boredom and pain of it, no less than in the

excitement and gladness: touch, taste, smell your way to the holy and hidden heart of it, because in the last analysis all moments are key moments, and life itself is grace."
Frederick Buechner

"This is the most full Emptiness I've ever experienced."
Adyashanti

APPENDIX 1:

Seven Steps to Peace

I n addition to the exercises of this book, I've found the seven statements below to be potent doorways back to true Being. The statements are meant to be read with an openness that allows us to sense into them. Reading them upon waking and upon going to bed and several more times through the day greatly stabilizes a person in true Being.

1. Disarmed, without effort or manipulation, I tune in to the true self.
2. Suffering is caused by believing my thoughts and can be relieved by questioning my thoughts.
3. I am the space through which experience passes. Peace is my natural state.
4. I sense that which takes delight in each moment even when my personality may not.

5. I open to that which requires nothing beyond what is given and engages without attachment.

6. I allow myself to live from the space of "I don't know."

7. I relax as the living pulse of being, as the essence of experiencing.

APPENDIX 2:

Byron Katie's "Judge Your Neighbor Worksheet" and Instructions (from thework.com)

F ill in the blanks below, writing about someone (dead or alive) you haven't yet forgiven one hundred percent. Use short, simple sentences. Don't censor yourself--try to fully experience the anger or pain as if the situation were occurring right now. Take this opportunity to express your judgements on paper.

1. Who angers, confuses, saddens, or disappoints you, and why? What is it about them that you don't like? I am _____ at _____ because _____ _____.

2. How do you want them to change? What do you want them to do? I want _____ to _____
   _____.

3. What is it that they should or shouldn't do, be, think, or feel? What advice could you offer?
   _____ should/shouldn't _____
   _____.

4. What do they need to do in order for you to be happy? I need _____ to _____ _____
   _____ .

5. What do you think of them? Make a list. _____
   is _____
   _ _____.

6. What is it that you don't want to experience with that person again? I don't ever want to _____
   _____
   _____.

The Four Questions (apply to each answer above)

1. Is it true?

2. Can you absolutely know that it's true.

3. How do you react, what happens, when you believe that thought?

4. Who would you be without the thought?

Turn the thought around

a) to the opposite

b) to the self

c) to the other

And find three genuine, specific examples of how each turnaround is true in your life.

Instructions

NOTICE: Who or what upsets you? Why? Recall a specific situation. To begin, relax and be still. Travel in your mind to a specific situation where you were angry, hurt, sad, or disappointed with someone. Witness the situation. Be there now. Notice, name, and feel the emotion you were experiencing at that time. Find the reason you were upset.

WRITE: Capture your stressful thoughts on a Judge-Your-Neighbor Worksheet using short, simple sentences. Staying anchored in the situation, at a specific moment in time, write down your responses to the questions on the Worksheet, using short, simple sentences. Write without censoring yourself. Allow yourself to be as judgmental, childish, and petty as you were in that moment. This is an opportunity to discover the cause of your stress and emotions in that moment.

QUESTION: Isolate one thought. Ask the four questions. Allow the genuine answers to arise. To being isolate a statement for inquiry. Now apply the four questions. Begin by repeating the original statement, then ask yourself each question. This Work is a meditation practice. It's like diving into yourself. Contemplate the questions, one at a time. Drop into the depths of yourself, listen, and wait. The answer will meet your question.

TURN IT AROUND: Turn the thought around. Is the opposite as true as or truer than the original thought? To do the turnarounds, find the opposites of the original statement on your Worksheet. Often a statement can be turned around to the self, to the other, and to the opposite. Not every statement as as many as three turnarounds. Some may have just one or two, and others may have more than three. Some turnarounds may not make sense to you. Don't force these.

Acknowledgments

I am ever grateful for every person in my life as they are all my teachers. I have been supported by my family and friends, partners, teachers, managers, colleagues, clients, and neighbors.

About Lisa's Life Experiences

Lisa is often available for questions. Some have asked about her life experiences. As a child, she had spiritual experiences with "God" in the framework of Christianity, and focused on spiritual growth as a paramount interest. She grew up in a military family. She excelled in school and earned a Bachelors degree in Mathematics and English, then an M.S. in Chemical Engineering and worked for a few Fortune 100 companies. She earned an MBA while she was working and transitioned into medical product management. She continued graduate studies in divinity and then in psychology. After 12 years, she left the corporate world to study human relating and sexuality and coached people and led retreats in these areas. In parallel, she was introduced to the practice of being present and was influenced by teachers like Adyashanti, Byron Katie, A.H. Almaas, Leonard Jacobson, Isaac Shapiro, and Gangaji. From time to time, she has had mild paranormal experiences. She later earned a degree in diagnostic medical ultrasound, which she continues to enjoy as her financial employ. She was first married at age 21 then divorced at age 33 and married again at age 48, both to loving partners. She's travelled throughout the U.S., Mexico, South America, and Europe as well as visiting Turkey, Israel, and Russia. She lives with her husband in a small coastal town in the hiking paradise of northern California. She can be reached at experiencingthetrueself.com.

Sept 24 21

THINGS ARE JUST AS THEY ARE

THINGS ARE IMPERMANENT

JOY AND SORROW ARISE AND PASS AWAY

ALL BEINGS ARE HEIRS of THEIR

INTENTIONS AND ACTIONS

MY JOY AND MY SORROW DEPEND UPON

MY INTENTIONS AND ACTIONS

NOT UPON THE WISHES of OTHERS

FOR ME

Made in the USA
Las Vegas, NV
17 September 2021